Mama Bear
to America's Marginalized

My Journey Through Foster Care and Adoption

Julie Reed McKissick

Wind
IN THE
REEDS
PRESS

Wind in the Reeds Press
172 Calvin Road
Cinebar, WA 98533
www.windinthereedspublishing.com

10. 9. 8. 7. 6. 5.

ISBN — 978-1-7349176-2-8

This book is dedicated to America's foster children. Keep fighting with courageous perseverance. Prove the discounters wrong. Show them you matter and that you are our future.

Table of Contents

You are a Well

Jeff Reed

You are a well
Water runs deep
Travelers can tell
Here they can sleep
They can lay down their things
And draw from your pool
Your water brings
needed renewal.

You are a stream
Water runs swift
Travelers can dream and
Let their thoughts drift
They can lay down their cares
And dangle their feet
Get lost in their stares
And imaginings sweet.

You are a lake
Water is calm
Travelers can take
time to belong
They can stroll on your shores
Skip stones at a chance
Watch sunset colors
shimmer and dance.

Introduction

Religion that God our Father accepts as pure and faultless is this: to look after orphans and widows in their distress and to keep oneself from being polluted by the world.

--James 1:27

The more I discover about my biological origins, the more I realize how my story mirrors that of the traumatized children my husband and I have fostered as well as the troubled teens I have taught. My passion is to offer hope and healing to hurting, forgotten children. I hope that my book provides America's marginalized children a voice and sparks a flame in others to join me on this journey.

*Please note that most names in this book have been altered to protect privacy.

PART ONE
Beginning

My Adoption

My journey began in the summer of 1968 when my biological mother, Ruth, was living alone in Northern California and anxiously looking for a way to support herself. She had no one on whom to depend and was looking for a job other than the periodic singing bit she would be lucky to land in a local bar. A good looking, charming stranger invited Ruth back to his apartment one night and promised her a job. She tried calling him the following week but was unsuccessful. A few weeks later, she also found out she was pregnant again.

Out of desperation, Ruth decided to briefly return to her ex-husband and five children in El Paso, Texas. However, she had to decide about the baby quickly developing inside of her. Ruth knew she was incapable of caring for this sixth baby; after all, she had abandoned all the others. She also saw obvious indicators of neglect and abuse of her older children by their father. Her ex suggested she get an abortion. Ruth's conclusion, however, was that she wanted to do something better this time; maybe she could give this baby a chance at a different kind of life.

Ruth secretly contacted the Lee Moore Christian Children's Home in El Paso, Texas with a request for a Christian couple to adopt her baby girl as soon as she was born and told the foster agency that the baby's father was "unknown". Paperwork was completed and the wait for my unceremonious arrival into this world began.

I was born two months prematurely and weighed a mere three pounds. Although, many years later, Ruth told me that she

13

knew I would be alright the day she walked away from me in the maternity ward at the hospital; as she peered at me through the nursery window, I was the baby screaming the loudest.

A social worker placed little me in a foster family's home for 2 months, to make sure I was going to thrive. There was some concern that my head appeared overly large for my body. All possible joking aside, the visiting nurse was afraid I might have "water on the brain," or meningitis. Thankfully, after multiple measurements of my head, my body grew more proportionally and I became eligible for adoption.

Meanwhile, a U.S. Army Chaplain, Major John Reed, and his wife, Lillian, were excitedly waiting for a phone call from the children's home about a baby girl. They had three healthy sons, Brad, Jeff and Greg, but were unable to have any more children naturally and had always desired a daughter.

After waiting for six months, the Reeds finally received the call they had been anticipating. John and Lil were told that a baby girl was available; they could come see her at the children's home if they wished to consider her for their own. However, Lil responded that she did not need to come see the baby first. No, she and her husband would be coming immediately to pick her up and take their new baby girl home. Of course, that day changed my life forever. Me, an abandoned, tiny little nobody, suddenly became a cherished somebody with a name. Any positive impact I have made, any heart I have touched, any contribution to society I have been blessed to give in my home or career, have all been made possible because John and Lil stepped out on a ledge, took a chance, and adopted me.

Brad, Jeff, Greg, and Julie Reed

My parents had to wait one year for permanency with monthly visits from a social worker who continued to measure my head to see if it was growing properly. My mom said that she felt as if she was on pins and needles for those 12 long months, worried that social services would take me away from them due to my medical concerns. Finally, John and Lilly wrote a check to the foster agency for $500.00 and obtained my new birth certificate. I was officially, "Julie Ann Reed"!

Although still only a tenuous five pounds when I first joined the Reed family at two months old, I quickly gained weight because I was receiving the physical and emotional affection essential for all babies to thrive. In other words, I was a fortunate child, indeed; I finally had a <u>real</u> mother and father.

Sometimes, curious, tactless people innocently have asked me if I know my "real" mother or "real" father. I always respond, "Of course I do; they raised me!"

As a young mom, I discovered the story, <u>The Velveteen Rabbit</u> (Bianco & Graham 1996). It describes "realness" perfectly:

"What is REAL?" asked the Velveteen Rabbit one day... "Does it mean having things that buzz inside you and a stick-out handle?"

"Real isn't how you are made," said the Skin Horse. "It's a thing that happens to you. When [someone] loves you for a long, long time, not just to play with, but REALLY loves you, then you become Real."

"Does it hurt?" asked the Rabbit.

"Sometimes," said the Skin Horse, for he was always truthful. "When you are Real you don't mind being hurt."

"Does it happen all at once, like being wound up," he asked, "or bit by bit?"

"It doesn't happen all at once," said the Skin Horse. "You become. It takes a long time. That's why it doesn't often happen to people who break easily, or have sharp edges, or who have to be carefully kept.

"Generally, by the time you are Real, most of your hair has been loved off, and your eyes drop out and you get loose in the joints and very shabby. But these things don't matter at all, because once you are Real you can't be ugly, except to people who don't understand... once you are Real, you can't become unreal again. It lasts for always."

My parents never treated me differently than my three older brothers, their naturally born children, in terms of "belonging". I have never felt loved any less. In fact, my oldest brother, Brad, would tell you that I was a bit spoiled being the only girl and youngest in our family. My mom told me that I was their "...chosen child, born not of her womb, but of her heart."

Nonetheless, there were times in my childhood that I unexplainably did feel different than my adoptive family members. For instance, many nights after dinner, I would loudly and happily sing and dance all over the kitchen while my parents quietly focused on cleaning the dishes. I was definitely a mischievous and "free spirit". Additionally, I have always loved animals with a passion; this is certainly not true for my parents. However, my mom never tried to shape me into her image. I have countless memories of her giggling and saying, "Oh Julie, you are so fun." She has always celebrated our differences, instead of criticizing and trying to control me. She was a wise and gentle (and I am sure often exhausted) mother of four.

A children's book I highly suggest on the topic of adoption and "feeling different" as an adoptive child, is *Stellaluna,* by Janell Cannon. It is an engaging story in which a baby bat accidentally falls into a bird's nest one day. The mother bird allows Stellaluna to join her family, but expects her to act like a bird. The little bat tries very hard to act like her siblings, but finally accepts one day that she is just a bat.

John and Lil explained my adoption to me as a toddler through a book titled, <u>The Chosen Baby</u> (Wasson 1950). The pages have yellowed and the paper protective cover has gone missing, but the book still has an honored place upon my bookshelf today. In fact, every so often, I carefully take it out and glance through the pages. It still magically brings a smile to my face and elicits feelings of being special and dearly loved.

I really cannot remember a specific moment that my parents explained my adoption; I just always knew. I have met adoptive parents who were waiting to tell their children or had decided not to tell them at all. Each circumstance and child are unique. However, I would encourage parents to speak openly about the subject when their children are very young, so that the topic feels natural and normal as possible. It is certainly not something to be avoided or ashamed of, since the child had no say in the matter. On the other hand, there could be circumstances which warrant not informing a child of an adoption, such as safety concerns related to the birth family.

Somehow, my parents were able to communicate feelings of "being special" or "chosen" to me clearly in terms of my adoption and I absorbed them as my own. In fact, one afternoon, when I was four years old and we lived in a high-rise apartment building in New York City, two twin, four-year old terrors yelled down at me from their window, "Julie's adopted! Julie's adopted!"

The boys' mother later informed my mom that I turned around, looked up at them, and yelled back, "Yeah, and that makes me special!" I guess I have always been a spitfire. I think perhaps God gifted me with a fighting spirit not only so I could survive my infancy but knew I would need it in helping other children in their journeys.

Adoptees' Feelings

Although I usually associate my adoption with feelings of being special and loved, I have met other adoptees who painfully struggle with negative feelings about their adoptions. I have determined that these feelings are most often a result of their differing prenatal experiences, personalities, and home environments. Compounding these emotions can be a general stigma of shame and an unspoken message that adopted children should not talk openly. Afterall, they were the lucky ones and should be grateful that they were adopted by parents who wanted them. Nonetheless, it is crucial that adopted persons recognize and work through their feelings so that they can sustain healthy relationships in adulthood. The most common feelings I have discovered adopted children share and struggle with include: SHAME, REJECTION, ANXIETY, and MISTRUST.

Shame is a hidden, powerful ravager of our emotions. It makes a person feel innately flawed by releasing stress or anxiety hormones which then inescapably result in feelings of unworthiness (American Adoptions, Inc 2020). Not only that, but it can lead to withdrawal from others or addictions in an attempt to hide from the intense pain (Lamia 2011). Adopted children might feel this shame because they erroneously blame themselves for being abused and abandoned by their birth parents.

Although adoptees were wanted and shown permanent love by their adoptive parents, they can often be plagued by feelings of **rejection** throughout their lives. Plenty of evidence reveals that babies' brains are imprinted with their mothers' emotions inside the womb (De Victoria 2018). Therefore, even before they are born, babies are aware of whether or not their mothers wanted them. Feelings of rejection can increase when they are informed about their past and discover that their biological mothers willingly gave them away. Furthermore, curious people can exacerbate these feelings when they ask insensitive questions of an adopted child or adult, such as, "How could your mother do that?!" It is important to teach adopted children to be careful with whom they share their life stories and that it is their right to simply respond, "I would rather not discuss it; let's talk about something else," if they feel like it. On the other hand, children should talk about their feelings with someone they trust who is objective and does not have their own personal feelings invested.

Anxiety is an inherent reaction of adopted children to the lack of control they have had over so many elements of their lives. They are subconsciously reacting to the collection of all of the unknown puzzle pieces of their biological past and how many times they moved between their birth parents and various foster families before they were finally placed in a permanent home. In fact, children who experience multiple placements are unfortunately at a higher risk of developing behavioral, emotional, and academic difficulties as they get older, especially if they do not receive therapeutic intervention (Rubin, Oreilly, Luan, & Localio 2007).

Sometimes an unintended response to the shame, rejection and anxiety foster or adopted children can feel is **mistrust** of others which can then lead to difficulty developing long term relationships with others. The two people, dad and mom, who were supposed to be there for them at the beginning of their lives, were the very ones who did not meet their basic needs, or worse, subjected them to suffering. Of course, the levels of feelings of mistrust can also be dependent on the age of the children when they were adopted.

I will never forget an impactful story my husband and I heard in one of our foster parent training classes. The social worker told us about a baby, only a few months old, who was failing to thrive with his biological parents. The infant was refusing to eat; he was starving himself. He was eventually removed from his home by the Department of Child and Family Services (DCFS), and placed in the home of loving foster parents where he started eating, smiling, and flourishing. At age one, a judge decided it was time to reunify the baby boy with his birth parents. Monthly visits by a county social worker followed who found that the baby was shutting down and starving himself again. That little baby incredibly made the decision at age one that his birth parents were not trustworthy; he had no control over the situation, so he decided not to eat. In this case, the social worker quickly intervened, informed the judge, and the baby was permanently placed back with his foster parents who finally adopt him. Unfortunately, it has been my lifetime experience that most foster babies spend a lifetime of being pulled in and out of their biological families. This foster baby's judge and county worker truly were outliers in the maelstrom of the child welfare system. I, in fact, consider them heroes.

For obvious reasons, I am a strong advocate of adoption. However, I would also be remiss if I did not warn potential adoptive parents that beyond normal feelings related to being adopted, due to factors such as genetics or prenatal exposure to drugs, there is the possibility that their adopted children will have struggle with more serious mental health issues. For example, I felt deeply saddened for the adoptive parents of several of my students when I was teaching teen girls diagnosed with Emotional Disturbance (ED). One infertile couple who had joyfully adopted their daughter as a newborn baby, were now, when she was 15 years old, inexplicably having to deal with her erratic and dangerous behaviors on a daily basis. While at school, the girl was able to maintain self-control and follow our strict routine well. Conversely, when she went home every afternoon, my student displayed out of control behavior to the point of threatening her own adoptive parents in their bed with a kitchen knife.

Therefore, I encourage prospective adoptive parents to investigate, ask many questions, and educate themselves; be hopeful, yet not naive. Some adopted children will be amazingly healthy and fairly easy to raise, with all the normal ups and downs any child experiences. On the other hand, others will require intense counseling and support. To be fair, sometimes adoption agencies are not provided with a great deal of pertinent information from biological parents, such as their mental health or addiction history. There are also times adoption agencies will withhold certain facts about a child's background from potential adoptive parents in order to increase the chances for the child of being adopted (Park 2010). However, I can thankfully say that I have recently observed firsthand a new trend in this area of disclosure. In the attempt at avoiding multiple placements and foster or adoptive children being returned to social services, social workers are starting to provide more facts about a child upfront.

Adoptive parents' attitudes and actions can tremendously impact how their children process their own feelings about being adopted. Parents have the power to normalize adoption and their children's ambiguous feelings by reading books on adoption, such as, *Tell Me Again About the Night I Was Born* (Curtis 1998), and practicing being comfortable with their children's questions. Parents can assist their children in accepting their adoption positively by purposefully bringing up the subject themselves periodically. An openness about talking about their adoption can lead to a more positive identity for adopted children (American Adoptions, Inc 2020). Some children may need purposeful assistance in processing their deeply embedded thoughts and feelings. One way or another, those feelings will surface in an adopted child at some point; if parents prepare themselves ahead of time on how they are going to respond to their child, then it will benefit everyone.

Nonetheless, there are certainly going to be surprises in adopting a child for which parents have no way to prepare. For instance, a close friend of mine, Sherry, and her husband adopted their oldest daughter, Amy, as an eighteen-month-old toddler from an orphanage in China. Amy displayed seething anger and resisted bonding with her parents from the first day of her arrival in the United States, even to the point of hitting and intentionally urinating on her adoptive mother. Nonetheless, Sherry and her husband continued to pray and seek understanding of their little girl; they never gave up. Sherry told Amy continuously that she loved her and attempted holding her tightly during tantrums over and over again.

Finally, one day, when Amy was just three years old, while throwing a fit, she suddenly screamed at Sherry, "You left me!" Her mother reassured her daughter that she had never left her and never would. Yet, Amy yelled back, "Yes you did; you are a liar!"

It was at that moment that my friend realized that she needed to tell little Amy about her Chinese biological mother.

Using simple words, she told the 3-year-old that her mother in China had carried Amy in her tummy but was unable to keep her and brought her to a place where Amy would be cared for and get a new family. After hearing this, the little girl's hostile behavior immediately ceased and she appeared stunned; after asking many questions, Amy started to sob and hugged her mother.

After several hours of crying, my dear friend asked her daughter, "Can I be your mommy?"

Amy responded, "Yes." This was the beginning of healing and building trust for this family. However, their little girl would continue to struggle trusting others outside of her immediate family and some of her emotional issues would intensify in her teen years.

My friend, Sherry, admitted to me that she entered the adoption process with a great deal of idealism; she believed she and her husband possessed everything necessary to raise their oldest adoptive daughter into a well-adjusted adulthood. She had no idea how her sensitive daughter's perceived abandonment would continually play out in her emotional and social development, later resulting in deep-seated layers of self-protection. Sherry felt totally unprepared; no one had warned her how her daughter's emotional struggles, later identified as Attachment Disorder, would sometimes disrupt the entire family, and even alienate them from friends and family who were unwilling to accept her eldest daughter's challenges. However, as a result of this difficult process, Sherry also discovered that she could let go of her concern for what others thought and her fear of failure to instead focus on loving her daughter and nurse her healing one-step-at-a-time.

Interestingly, my friend's other two daughters, although they had been through similar childhood experiences as their older sister, Amy, did not respond in the same manner. The other girls easily bonded with their adoptive parents almost immediately. All adopted children find their own unique ways to cope with their past and their resulting feelings, both consciously and subconsciously. However, honest and open communication fostered by their parents will go a long way towards assisting them in this process.

Meeting My Birth Family

Although I did not view my adoption status as negative, I did struggle with coming to terms with my self-identity growing up, as is natural for many adoptees. I knew very little about my biological parents, but as a teenager, I started making up things about them in my imagination. This curiosity about my biological family would lead me to pursue meeting them one day.

It was not until I was 27 years old that I decided to search for my birth family. Inquisitiveness was certainly a major factor in this decision, but I was also about to give birth to my first child and wanted to know some medical history. There are those people who choose to never search out answers to their genealogical past. I think I waited until I was older, because I did not want to hurt my adoptive mother's feelings. My adoptive father was always pragmatic; it was pretty hard to hurt his feelings. My mother, on the other hand, tended to react anxiously whenever the subject of my birth mother arose.

The process of finding half of my birth family turned out to be an easy process for me. I called the Lee Moore Children's Home in El Paso, Texas, and asked if someone there could provide me with information about my bio family; the receptionist positively told me that someone would get back to me soon. A few days later, a social worker from the adoption agency called me and said that she had contacted my biological mother and siblings by phone to ask them if they were okay with releasing their names and phone numbers to me, so that I could reach out to them. They had all given her their consent. My biological father was not contacted, because the agency had no information on him, and I really did not know who he might be. At the time, my birth mother told me that my father could be one of three men she had been dating.

Over the course of the following week, I called my birth mother and four siblings to introduce myself and ask them a few questions. I felt both excited and awkward, because they were virtual strangers after all. Yet, I was thankful that they were open to getting to know me a little and did have the chance to ask about my family's medical history. Sadly, I never got to meet one of my older brothers, because he had died in drug-related circumstances when he was just 18 years old. My mother told me that the police found his body in a park in Houston, Texas.

At that time, I was teaching full-time at a non-public school (NPS), on the grounds of the David & Margaret Home in La Verne, California. This was originally an orphanage for boys and girls during World War Two, but in the 1970s became a residential facility for teen girls from the Department of Children and Family Services (DCFS), or the juvenile probation system. As a result of all of the experiences I had with my students and their backgrounds, I was not expecting a fairy tale in terms of what I learned about my birth family. Nevertheless, I really had no details on what I would discover.

The story I heard from my mother and siblings on the telephone over the following year about the time leading up to my birth and adoption, was both a tragedy and a miracle. Each of them supplied a different piece of my pre-adoption story puzzle. My birth mother, Ruth, informed me that she had decided to give me up for adoption because she had not felt able to care for me and that she had knowledge of abusive behavior on the part of her ex towards her five other children.

Ruth also admitted that since she had three different boyfriends at the time of my conception, she could not prove beyond a shadow of a doubt that I had the same father as my siblings. However, from details that I would later learn from one of my sisters, I erroneously concluded that there were too many coincidences for me to not have the same father. That is what I believed for the next 25 years until I found out the truth while writing this book.

My oldest sister, Karen, showed the most interest in getting to know me, at least initially. She told me about herself and her son. Karen told me that I should not try to meet our birth father because he abused them, including locking them in a closet for three days. She also kindly asked me questions about my life and adoptive family and said she was very happy for me. Surprisingly, Karen even called my adoptive mother and father one evening to thank them for caring for me. She explained to me that she blamed our mother for their father's abuse, because she had repeatedly abandoned them. Karen painted a memory of our mother unexpectedly showing up one day and giving her a bicycle for her birthday, but then disappearing again. She also told me of a third-grade teacher who taught her how to comb her hair and groom herself for the first time. Furthermore, my sister said that she and her three living siblings were all geographically spread out and did not have much contact with one another. She said she would like to meet me in person someday. Karen also warned me not to give our mother any money. By the way, my biological mother has never asked me for any money over the two decades we have been in touch.

I also met my oldest biological brother, Luke, over the phone. He was friendly, but we lost contact with one another eventually. Luke struggled with mental illness and would end up living on the streets of various cities in Texas. Karen, in fact, told me once that both she and our brother, Luke, had been diagnosed with Bipolar Disorder, but that she later determined that they both were on the Autism Spectrum.

Obviously, there were some surprises for me in meeting my birth family, but one of them actually came from myself. I unexpectedly felt guilt building up inside of me once I heard about the suffering my siblings had endured. I was explicitly made aware of what God had spared me from in allowing me to be adopted by John and Lil Reed, loving Christian parents. On the other hand, I firmly believed my five birth siblings were also loved by God. So, I asked myself why I was spared neglect, abuse, and emotional harm and they were not. I could not manufacture an answer and felt a profound grief for my siblings' lost childhood. I wondered if perhaps God knew I would not have survived if I had stayed with them, or maybe He had a plan for me to serve others like my siblings.

Over the course of a brief telephone conversation with my second oldest biological sister, Lana, she informed me that she was living with her husband in a midwestern state and had a good job. I also learned that she had decided to never have children. Moreover, Lana said that she had a different view of our father than our sister, Karen, so she did not want to talk about him. Lana ended up living with her dad for the last months of her life as she lay dying of breast cancer.

Finally, I spoke with my youngest brother, Matt, who was just two years older than me. He was married and had three little girls. I learned that he was living near our mother in Texas and had some contact with her, but none with our siblings. He asked me a few questions and answered some of mine, but that was the extent of our contact. It was clearly obvious to me that my brother did not reciprocate my desire to get to know him.

Ever tenacious, I attempted in the following years to make more contacts with Matt, but finally gave up after a trip my daughter, Alisa, and I took to New York City. By the time of that trip, Matt and his family had moved one hour outside of NYC and we made plans to meet there in person. My anticipation of the meeting left me both nervous and excited as my daughter and I traversed the hot sightseeing spots. However, at the exact moment that I was gazing up at the light blue colossal Statue of Liberty, after we had taken a ferry ride over to Liberty Island, I received a disappointing call from Matt. He told me that he was not going to be making the drive into the city to meet with me, but hoped we enjoyed the rest of our stay.

After about one year of some sporadic phone calls, I planned an actual trip to Texas to meet my biological family face to face. My mother and two sisters agreed to make plans to travel to meet me on a designated day we agreed upon; I never met my brothers in person. Lil, my adoptive mom, offered to go with me on the momentous trip, but although I thought it nice of her to offer, I wanted to do it alone without the complication of needing to worry about her feelings too. I took our daughter, Alisa, then age 1-½, with me on a plane ride from Los Angeles, California, to Houston, Texas, one sunny summer day.

Ruth, my birth mother, met me and my daughter at our hotel. We spent a little time together as she asked me to listen to her sing a few songs and read some of the poems she had written. I discovered that she and I shared a love of music, singing, and animals, but not much else. Basically, Ruth and I were strangers, except for the undeniable and weighty fact that she gave birth to me.

Ruth also told me, "At least I did one good thing in my life; giving you up for adoption was the right thing to do." She admitted that she felt shame over her abandonment of her other five children, but that she had also been abused as a young child and just did not have the ability to raise children. I can clearly remember, as Ruth spoke, my 1-½ year old, beautiful, sweet daughter, Alisa, sitting on the carpet of that hotel room playing quietly. I was astounded that my biological mother never touched or asked to hold Alisa, her own granddaughter. She did not ask me any questions about my life on that trip either, but her happiness that I had come to see her was clear.

That evening, I drove Ruth and Alisa in my rental car to a nearby restaurant to connect with my two older sisters, Karen and Lana. I was astonished and grateful to discover that Karen had driven 18 straight hours with her eleven-year-old son from New Mexico to meet me! However, I also had no idea how awkward that dinner was going to turn out to be.

I had felt so excited to get to see and know my sisters, at least a little, but Lana talked nonstop and glared at our mother over the course of the entire meal. Ruth, our mother, quickly became defensive and sulked. Karen, the eldest sibling, tried to interject a few comments and questions my way, but any meaningful conversation was pretty much impossible. We ended up parting ways at the end of the meal; that was the first and last time I saw my sisters.

Nevertheless, my toddler daughter and I stayed a few more days in Houston and spent some pleasant time with my birth mother chatting, touring the area. and going out to eat. When people find out that I am adopted, they often ask if I look like my birth mother. Honestly, I did not recognize much of a resemblance to her. On the other hand, I was pleased to finally discover that she was the source of our daughter's cute little button nose.

A few days after returning to California after my trip to Texas, I called my oldest sister, Karen, and told her that I was disappointed about how the dinner had gone. She chastised me and said that I should be more compassionate towards our sister, because Lana could not stand to be around our mother. In fact, going to that dinner had been very hard on Lana. I apologized, but privately wished that one of them had told me about that before my visit, so that we could have met up in a separate location from our mother. Unfortunately, that chance was gone. I simply had to accept that some of the missing pieces of my past were lost.

I spoke with my siblings a handful of times on the telephone after that, but the interest on both sides gradually faded. We shared a genetic past, but little else. Conversely, Ruth, my birth mother, and I, have maintained infrequent contact via telephone calls and birthday cards. I do not feel emotionally close to Ruth, but I do care for her well-being, pray for her, and am grateful that she safely carried me in her womb for seven months in order to give me a chance at life. I am also thankful that she sought a better life for me and gave me up for adoption.

At the conclusion of writing the first rough draft of this book, in the Spring of 2020, I had the urge to dig a little deeper into my past and try to find out the true identity of my biological father. My daughter and I had registered with Ancestry.com several years previous, but I had not checked on it. On a whim, I decided to try using a different genetic history service, 23 and Me, to see if I got any different results. To summarize, I did discover a first cousin in Northern California, who informed me that her dad and his brother were only siblings. That meant that her dad's brother had to be my bio dad! She then asked her mother to send me an old photo of my dad and a newspaper article about his death.

After I saw the picture of my birth father, Ross (Roosevelt) Williams, I had no doubts; I looked just like him. I was shocked, to say the least. It was an unexplainable feeling to finally look like someone else. Not only that, but the news article revealed that Ross was brutally murdered. At age 43, he was stabbed 15 times inside his apartment building in Northern California; the murder was never solved. Suddenly, I found myself oddly grieving for the awful demise of a father whom I never met. I also believe that he never knew I existed.

Julie Reed McKissick   *Ross (Roosevelt) Williams*

The good news is that my cousin got me in contact with my half-sister (from the same dad), Jennifer, who was 59 years old and lived in Colorado Springs, Colorado. She was thrilled to have contact with me, so I planned a plane trip last November 2020, with my husband and our two adult children. We shared an early Thanksgiving dinner with my sister, her boyfriend, her two daughters (her two sons were out of state), and seven of her eleven grandchildren! I was pleased to discover that my sister and I resemble one another and share many personality traits, such as dynamic energy and strong-willed spirits. In fact, my husband mentioned that he wondered if he should warn the Chamber of Commerce in Colorado Springs that my energetic sister and I would be in the same location at the same time.

One of the best surprises I was gifted with that day was when I met Loganne, my five-year old great niece, for the first time. I had to look twice; she looked just like me and my daughter, Alisa, at her age! Everyone was amazed. I showed her parents old pictures on my cell phone of my daughter and myself and they all agreed. All the other children were fair and had blond hair; Loganne's parents had no idea of the origin of her appearance. They also said she was a real "stinker". That was just icing on the cake for me. I laughed aloud and responded, "Well, you now know who she looks like. I can also promise you that her strong spirit will come in handy one day. She will turn out just fine".

By the way, Jennifer and I know that we also have multiple biological brothers somewhere too, but we have not been able to locate them yet.

Julie and Jennifer

PART TWO
Fostering and Adopting

Jacob

Our 25-year-old son, Jacob, stopped by one evening a few weeks ago with his little Terrier mix, Oliver, to have dinner with us and pick-up his mail. I am not sure why he still gets his mail at our house and will not get a P.O. box. He says it is because he trusts us more than his apartment mates or neighbors, but I suspect it is just because he likes to keep a tangible tie with us. It does get him over to our home at least once a month.

Anyway, that night, Jake walked into the kitchen and out of the blue said, "I don't know why you guys adopted me; I had so many issues! I was so lucky."

I replied, "We love you, Jacob, and will always be here for you."

Although, I later reflected upon Jacob's interesting question: Why DID we adopt him? Let me take you back to where it all began. After our daughter, Alisa, was born, I was never able to get pregnant again. I was heartbroken and grieved for years to come over that evaporating dream.

Alisa was five years old when my husband and I started discussing and praying about the possibility of pursuing foster care and adoption. I not only experienced a never-ending urge to mother, but also spoke with Dave about the benefits for our daughter in having a sibling. Alisa would not only have a companion for the rest of her life, but would have to learn to get along with another child and share. We talked about international adoption, but settled upon staying within the L.A.

County; our decision was based upon my conviction that there were plenty of American children in need of a home and the fact that it would be a more affordable process.

The first step was to find a foster family agency (FFA) in our area which was also certified to approve adoptions. Dave and I found Serenity Infant Care Homes Foster Family Agency (Serenity), in Covina, California, a 10-minute drive from our home at the time in Glendora, CA. The polite woman on the phone asked us to attend an Orientation Class at their agency one night a few months later. Dave and I agreed and looked forward to hearing how we might welcome a sweet little baby into our family.

Once again, God had different plans than my own. At the orientation session at the FFA, we were sitting and listening quietly to a young foster mother share her experiences, when I noticed a little boy with dark brown hair playing with Matchbox cars behind her on the carpet in the corner. I could hear him repeating, seemingly in his own world, "Varoom, varoom, varoom." He appeared to me to be Hispanic, around five or six years old, and very cute. Like a restless bird, my thoughts took flight.

The following week, I called Serenity and asked to speak with a social worker; I was transferred to a woman named Naseem. I asked her about the little boy I had seen at the class the previous week. Naseem informed me that the five-year old's name was Jacob, he was Mexican American, and he was not doing well in his current foster home where he had lived with four other children for 1-½ years. Naseem elaborated further. Jacob had been born in El Paso, Texas (my same birth place; Go, Cowboys!), but his mother now lived in Denver, Colorado. He was a very active child who demanded a great deal of attention. Being the youngest of five children in his foster home, he was starting to get into trouble frequently and there was conflict. Moreover, Jacob's foster parents were looking into adopting a baby.

The social worker explained to me on the phone that although Jacob's mom, Angelina, lived in Colorado with his two younger siblings, she had been attending court dates in California. She was trying to get custody of her son back, but was having difficulty meeting the judge's expectations that she hold a steady job and have a safe, permanent home for her children. I also learned that Angelina gave birth to Jacob when she was just 14 years old, after her mother had kicked her out of her home and while wandering from place to place with her older boyfriend.

Jacob's mother and Jacob himself would later fill-in-the-blanks of Jacob's early story for me. After leaving her two infant daughters with a friend in Colorado, Angelina lost custody of him while on a trip to California with his father. A neighbor heard angry screaming and pans hitting the wall dividing their apartments. This lady had seen a little boy with them and decided to call the Department of Child and Family Services (DCFS) out of concern for his safety. DCFS showed up with a police officer soon afterwards and actually took both Jacob and his mother to a shelter in Los Angeles, because Angelina was only 18 years old.

It was not long before Jacob's mother took matters into her own hands, though, out of a need to get back to her two baby girls in Colorado. So, one afternoon, Angelina quietly threw her duffle bag over a wall and snuck out of the county placement with Jacob when no staff members were looking. DCFS labeled the teen mother a thief of her own little boy and filed a missing child report.

A few months later, there was a fire in Jacob's apartment in Denver, and the fire department and police were called. Jacob's presence and the L.A. County DCFS missing child report was discovered in the process and so a social worker and police officers showed up at Jacob's doorstep without warning. The terrified four-year-old boy was whisked away in the back of a black and white police car. That evening, Jacob took his first ride on an airplane with another social worker who delivered him to his first foster home in California. Years later, when Jacob would share these details of that fateful day with me, I could clearly understand how those traumatic events had an acutely negative impact on Jacob's view of law enforcement. Jacob, being emotionally immature, blamed the police for his fear.

Angelina saved money for several long bus rides to Los Angeles for her son's court appointments; she implored with the judge every time to give her son back to her. Unfortunately, she was unable to get her life circumstances together enough in Colorado to meet the judge's requirements. This was the reason Jacob remained in a foster home for two years with a very nice family, but where he was starting to show signs of dysfunction. Regardless of the causes which initially landed Jacob in foster care and the outcomes, I have been eternally grateful to Jacob's birth mother for fighting for him.

As Jacob's foster parents started making more negative comments and requesting a baby placement, his social worker at the FFA, Naseem, made appointments and took Jacob on some visits to a few potential adoptive parents. Nothing had worked out for the little boy yet. Jacob later described one of the visits to me. His foster dad dropped him off at the agency one morning and Naseem took him, "... on a really long car ride to a big home where a nice lady opened the door to us and invited us in. There was a big bowl of fruit and cookies on the table. I was really hungry, so I kept hoping the nice lady would offer me some of that food to eat, but she never did. I was confused and asked Naseem after we left the lady's home and got in her car, why we didn't get any of the fruit or cookies. She laughed and told me she didn't understand either, but would take me through a McDonald's drive through on the way back home."

After Dave and I saw Jacob at the foster parent orientation and heard his story, we asked Naseem about us fostering and possibly adopting Jacob. The social worker explained to us that the FFA was generally not allowed to move a child from one foster home to another due to the trauma caused to the child by multiple placements. On the other hand, since Jacob was not flourishing in his current situation, she would bring up our offer at their next staff meeting. So, we waited for their answer.

The FFA decided we could be a positive placement change for Jacob and told us that the next step in getting to know if he and our family would be a good match, was to have a weekend visit. Jacob would stay overnight with us. Naseem also told Jacob about our family and showed him our picture. She asked the little five-year old if he wanted to meet us and possibly live with us and he agreed.

One Friday afternoon in September, 2001, Naseem dropped Jacob at our front doorstep with his backpack filled with a few changes of clothes, his toothbrush, and some toys. The visit was positive; Jacob and Alisa got along well and nothing really out of the ordinary occurred. We played, ate meals together, attended a friend's birthday party, and went to church. On that Sunday afternoon, before Naseem picked Jacob up to take him back to his foster parents, he looked up at Dave and I like a fawn with his brown hair and blue eyes and innocently asked, "Was I good? Naseem told me that I better be good at your home or you won't want to keep me."

After looking at one another aghast, Dave and I reassured Jacob that, yes, he had been very good and that we all looked forward to seeing him again soon. I could only imagine what thoughts and pressure Jacob had been experiencing with us that weekend! However, upon later reflection, realized that Naseem knew Jacob and his behavioral challenges very well. She also genuinely cared about him and wanted him to have a good chance at being adopted.

Dave and I then needed to finish our certification process to become foster parents. This included many training hours learning about the needs of a traumatized child and expectations for foster parents, putting together first-aid and emergency kits, installing smoke detectors in all of the bedrooms, and child-proofing our home. Part of that last requirement was to lock away all of our garden tools, including rakes and shovels. We just could not picture a toddler or even a six-year-old picking up a shovel and banging us over the head when we were not looking. However, all sarcasm aside, we had to do whatever we were told if we wanted to foster Jacob. We also knew that the ultimate goal was child safety, even if we thought the county might have gone a little overboard. Each state has its own home approval process for foster parents, or "resource parents", as is the current term used. However, the checklist for the California Department of Social Services, can be found on the CDSS website under, "Resource Family Home Health and Safety Assessment Checklist" (or see the pdf link in my resources section at the end of this book).

This comprehensive certification process is probably one of the things that discourages some people the most from becoming foster/adoptive parents. Besides those steps, social workers also asked us endless invasive questions, such as the status of our sex life as a married couple. Basically, in becoming foster parents, we had to give up on our privacy to a large extent. My husband and I learned that keeping a sense of humor was crucial. On the other hand, years down the line, we would often wonder with a fair amount of anger, why foster parents were required to do so much to protect the children placed temporarily in our care, only to see children returned to parents in homes where the standards of care were extremely subpar.

Nonetheless, two months before Jacob's sixth birthday, in October, 2001, Dave and I passed a home inspection and were approved to welcome Jacob into our home. We had moved Alisa into a larger bedroom which we redecorated with purple and pink striped painted walls and prepared her previous bedroom for Jacob. Off came the Winnie-the-Pooh wallpaper and up went red and blue paint with sailboats. We never heard our daughter, Alisa, complain about the room change. Nevertheless, the first night Jacob moved in, after he had gone to sleep, I caught her with a big red marker silently writing her name in large, bold letters across the door of her old bedroom: "ALISA". I decided to let her finish, then told her she would have to wash it off (all the while laughing uproariously on the inside).

I recently asked Alisa if she remembered how she felt when Jacob first joined our family; she said that she initially felt jealous but was ultimately thankful to have a playmate and brother. That is highly understandable, since she was our only adored child for five years! However, marking her name on Jacob's door was the only sign of jealousy that I can remember her displaying. Alisa was an amazingly stoic, patient, and tolerant (sometimes too much in my opinion), sister. We would often tell her that she was going to be able to get along with anyone after being trained by her brother.

Not long ago, I also texted 24-year-old Jacob to ask if he remembered how he felt when he first came to our home and when he started calling us "Dad" and "Mom". I think it is best to hear it in his own words. This is what our son told me: *"Yes, I definitely remember* (that night)*! It was like a breath of fresh air. I didn't have anything; you guys gave me everything. I remember just having, like grandparents, was a big thing to me. I think it only took a couple of days until I was comfortable and calling you "Mom" and "Dad". You made it okay; I didn't live with people who told me it was okay to do that before. Like, IDK, I remember the love when I first stepped in your house, like you guys cared about me. I'd hide from Sam and Sally* (his previous foster parents), *to see if they really wanted me and they'd constantly forget me places. I think they were more focused on the babies, but I never did that with you guys, not once. I think it was two days before dad said it was okay to call you guys, "Mom" and "Dad"; it was right before dinner. That was also the first time really eating as a family for me; I never had that at all anywhere. You guys saved me."*

I was surprised by Jacob's in-depth response. I am not sure why I had not asked Jacob before how he felt about coming to live with us, but it was powerful to hear Jacob's perspective. Something else that I discovered in parenting Jacob through all stages of his childhood from age six to young adulthood is that the scared, anxious, forgotten little four-year-old (the age he was when he entered foster care), never really left. That little guy inside of him was constantly seeking reassurance, attention (any way he could possibly get it, both positively and negatively), and tangible displays of lasting love.

I can remember tucking Jacob into bed his first night with us and how it helped me to start developing an awareness of assumptions my husband and I might make with him, along with all of the myriad of "strange" changes he might have been experiencing which just seemed "normal" to our family. For instance, I loved Raggedy Ann and Andy as a child, and excitedly displayed an Andy doll on Jacob's dresser, but he did not share my feelings. As I leaned over Jacob to say, "Goodnight", he first said that I looked scary; my mascara had smudged all around my eyes like a racoon). Next, he asked if I would get rid of the scary clown doll on his dresser. He explained that he hated clowns, because he had watched the movie, *It,* at his last foster home. I quickly removed the Raggedy Andy doll, prayed with Jacob, and then left his bedroom door ajar.

Early on, I discovered that Jacob was addicted to candy and fast food. I discovered why at his first visit with his birth mother when she brought him a McDonald's Happy Meal and bouquet of Tootsie Roll suckers. Many times, after we had just eaten a meal at home, as soon as we drove by a fast food restaurant, Jacob would automatically shout out, "I'm hungry!" I happily indulged the kids' desire for French fries about once each week, but Jacob had to accept a new lifestyle at our home. It was obvious he did not enjoy my cooking, but did not complain. Jacob was especially resistant towards vegetables, but eventually learned to eat them. I did not force the issue with him; it would have been a giant power struggle. Instead, I placed one spoonful of veggies on Jacob's dinner plate and told him that he had to finish it if he wanted some dessert at the end of the meal. Ironically, before kale was "a thing", Jacob was the one in our family who always shoved the whole decorative piece in his mouth from his plate at restaurants when we went to nicer restaurants.

At almost six years old, Jacob did not know how to swim yet and was very nervous around a swimming pool; our 5-½ year old daughter already swam like a gleeful guppy. My husband and

I discovered later that the lack of swim lessons was pretty common for foster children. Obviously, this is a safety concern, but it can truly highlight social disparity too, such as at birthday parties or beachside vacations. We decided to start Jacob on swim lessons right away and he quickly developed greater ability and confidence.

Other things that were readily apparent to us about Jacob was his energy and trouble with focusing on anything that disinterested him. I desperately decided a few months after Jacob arrived that we needed some help and enrolled him in martial arts classes at Red Dragon Karate in Glendora, CA. Not only was he able to burn off loads of energy, build his self-confidence, and be drilled with the importance of focusing and respecting himself and others in the classes, but he also made some good friends. His sister and I later joined the karate studio as well; it was something we shared for the next 3 or 4 years.

Jacob still had extra energy at home that sometimes could wear down on our patience. I can remember when he was about seven years old, one night when I was trying to make dinner, telling him to run up and down the driveway 20 times as fast as he could; I cheered him on from the kitchen window. When Jacob was about 11 years old, he and our daughter went to an overnight youth group activity at church. Upon arriving to pick them and one of his friends up, everyone looked exhausted, except for our son. He ran out excitedly and showed my husband the prize he had won. My husband has always said that Jacob could probably win a *Survivor* television show contest, because he can go days without sleeping, eating, or going to the bathroom!

Additionally, Jacob constantly struggled with impulsivity as a child; he said and did things without thinking. Only two weeks after he joined our family, I took him, and our daughter to

McDonald's with a moms' group from church. I was sitting and chatting with the other moms while watching the children play in the indoor playland nearby when I suddenly and helplessly witnessed Jacob reach his fist through the netting and punch another little boy in the face. Of course, the boy started crying loudly, and shortly afterwards, his father was yelling at Jacob. I jumped up to intercede and then was being yelled at to teach my son better manners. I told the irate man that I was very sorry about what had happened but asked him to calm down. The angry dad ended up leaving with his son and I quickly left with my children soon afterwards.

Although sometimes learning things "the hard way", Jacob did have moments of triumph over his impulsivity which Dave and I praised and rewarded. For example, one day when he was about seven years old, Jacob and I were stepping out of the right side of our minivan after parking and within eight inches of us was a shiny, candy apple red, glorious Corvette. Jacob paused, looked at the car, looked up at me, then walked away and up onto the sidewalk curb nearby. Proudly, he looked up at me and said, "Mom, I didn't touch it! I wanted to, but I didn't!" I smiled and congratulated him profusely. Honestly, I had been tempted to touch it too though.

Emotions drove Jacob. For the most part, he was happy and full of boundless energy. On the flip side, he also had his fair share of angry tantrums at home and in public. Physical means of discipline, such as spankings, for foster children were not allowed, so Dave and I utilized timeouts and taking preferred items or activities away for age-appropriate intervals. I sought out counseling for Jacob so that he could get assistance in addressing his high-strung emotions and learn better social skills; he would end up getting help through the foster agency, at his schools, and from a kind child therapist, Dr. Aubrey Fine in Claremont, CA, who my husband referred to as "Santa Claus".

In response to Jacob's public tantrums, I also gladly rediscovered the effective "Vulcan Grip". The Vulcan Grip was a handy technique my dad used on me when I was a disobedient child. Named after the Vulcan character, Spock, on the 70's *Star Trek* television show, it is a magical method of using one's thumb and forefinger to activate the pressure point between the neck and shoulder blade to disable someone else. It leaves no marks and causes no physical damage, but potently activates nerves. I used it to cause Jacob to suddenly relax, giving me a chance to then whisk him and Alisa quickly out to our waiting minivan and back home.

Moreover, during the times Jacob threw his royal tantrums on the hardwood floor in the hallway at home, I would quietly stand near him and calmly say, "You can cry as long as you want, but at the end of this, I will win. I will always win Jacob, because I am your parent." I guess he thought I would eventually give in; I did not. I suppose you could say Jacob and I were truly meant for each other. I was as stubborn as he was, but I also wanted him to know that the adults in his life now were stable. He could count on us to provide the boundaries he needed to feel safe. Jacob might have acted like he wanted to be in control, but was actually testing us to see if he could really count on us. Basically, our son was learning he could trust a few select adults for the first time in his life.

Dave was fully willing to get involved in the discipline of our children, but sometimes felt at a loss at what to do. Figuring out how to deal with Jacob's misbehavior and high-strung emotions could be overwhelming. He tended to respond to our son by speaking with Jacob logically and repeating something he said if Jacob did not "get it" the first time. However, if Jacob entered into one of his emotional funks, then he stopped listening and Dave's talking to him just elevated his stress level; the result was that both of them got angrier and started arguing until one of them walked away from the other.

I began to suggest to Dave that he give Jacob some time and space to decompress from his emotional tailspins before he tried to talk with him. I learned from working with my students who had cognitive processing and emotional disorders, that children in a state of emotional turmoil are not actively listening because they are in a survivalist shutdown mode. Talking to them while they are in this condition is a waste of effort and will just aggravate them further. Jacob would often implode when either Dave or myself tried talking to him while he was upset or in trouble; this was quite a sight to see. Every inch of our son's body gradually grew tenser by the second. He lost all eye contact, was either mumbling or crying, and sometimes would start scratching himself or punching a hard object to the point of making himself bleed. Moreover, within a few short minutes, his nose might even start bleeding.

I think I was able to relate to Jacob and have greater patience with him, partially because I had also been a highly emotional, energetic, sneaky, and stubborn child at times. I did my best to apply many of the parenting techniques my dad had modeled, including giving our children choices when appropriate to avoid power struggles. For instance, my dad would give me and my three older brothers two choices of consequences for lying, swearing, or disobeying our curfews, etc.; however, both choices were ones with which he agreed. The result was that he gave us a sense of control while ensuring that we really ended up not only learning from our misbehavior, but also doing something he preferred.

Yes, my dad was clever in his discipline of his own children, so when Jacob joined our family, I suppose it was natural that he liked to give my husband and I parenting advice at times. I respected my dad's sage counsel, but finally told him, "Dad, I am 'John Jr.'; I have tried all of the techniques you taught us, but Jacob still has ongoing emotional and behavioral issues". I am not sure he could really accept that there was not going to be an easy or quick solution for Jacob's problems. This changed one weekend when my parents came into town from Arizona and offered to stay with our kids overnight for the first time to give Dave and I a chance to get away together.

After we came back from our overnight trip, my dad did not share a lot of details, but never gave me advice about our son again. My parents looked pretty exhausted and I think my dad finally "got it'"; there was not going to be an absolute fix for Jacob. It was going to be a long, challenging, and at times rewarding road with Jacob.

Our son was 11 years old when my husband and I finally came to this same realization for ourselves, that raising Jacob was going to demand the training required for a marathon, not a 50-yard dash. We had worked so hard and seen increments of improvement but remarked to one another that the maturation process for Jacob was often one step forward and two steps backward. Instead of hopelessness, our acceptance resulted in an incredible feeling of relief. We had a new agenda for our family: learning healthy ways for all of us to cope with Jacob's struggles, rather than resenting them. Instead of slaying the dragon, we were going to have to discover ways to tame it.

As a teacher, I saw this arduous battle for acceptance in many of the parents of my students with disabilities, especially those with more severe impairments. All loving parents desire that their children live normal, full, and happy lives. Children with disabilities can certainly attain happiness and purpose, but on a divergent and sometimes rockier path than that of their non-disabled peers. Be that as it may, instead of accepting the reality and limitations relevant for their children, parents can tend to seek an all-encompassing solution, get angry, and blame others. Eventually, however, healthy parents reach a point of acceptance regarding their children. They still advocate for growth, equity, and respect for their children, but take the road less traveled, a fresh path with less strife and attainable goals.

Along with acceptance, at some point, I stopped asking God for more patience and started asking Him to fill my husband and I with His unconditional love for Jacob. I focused on the Bible verse, I Peter 4:8: "Above all, love each other deeply, because love covers over a multitude of sins" (NIV). Dave and I eventually made our love for Jacob our beacon; it allowed us to not only persevere but bond as a family.

In addition to Jacob's struggles with anger, he exhibited almost constant fear when he first came to live with us. His most frequent question was, "Can I die from that?" Dave and I would have to frequently reassure him. It had reached a level of obsession for poor little six-year-old Jacob, but a benefit of his insecurities was that he always stayed very close to me whenever we went anywhere.

Due to our foster son's impulsivity, unstable emotions, challenges with processing information, previously moving to multiple schools, and originally having Spanish as his primary home language, Jacob struggled in school academically and socially starting in Kindergarten. Matter of fact, when he first came to live with us at almost six years old, Jacob could not spell his first name or tie his shoes. I made those skills a priority. At the end of First Grade, his teachers and I agreed that it would benefit Jacob to repeat First Grade in order to allow him extra time to strengthen his emotional maturity and fledgling academic skills.

Conversely, Jacob's gross motor skills were strong. He easily picked-up new sports. Case in point, one Saturday, during the summer, Dave took Jacob and our daughter, Alisa, to the beach to teach them to surf. Jacob got up on the board on his first try.

Unfortunately, Dave and I received frequent phone calls from Jacob's elementary school; it felt like we were holding our breath, waiting for the next emergency to occur. One morning, when Jacob was in First Grade, I received a call at work from his school that Jacob had been crying for more than an hour. I requested to leave work early. When I arrived at Jacob's school, I found him sitting alone at a table outside his classroom, still sniffling. I hugged him and asked him why he was crying. He said something about another student making fun of him; I calmly told him it was time to stop crying and he did.

In the first few years of Jacob living with us, I was teaching part-time at a school for teen girls with learning and emotional disabilities. I also had a Special Education teaching credential and was taking classes working towards my Masters of Special Education. These educational and professional experiences turned out to be a great pairing with Jacob's needs. One Saturday, I attended a conference at which a speaker presented on the topic of Attention Deficit Disorder (ADD). One statement she made that day changed my entire perspective and approach with Jacob. She loudly proclaimed to us all, "Stop asking your children or students with ADD the question, WHY? Why did you do that? Why are you doing that? Impulsive children don't know WHY they do the things they do; they just do them." It was such a simple, yet profound principle.

The more I reflected on the frustrating interactions my husband and I had with Jacob, the more I realized that we had often asked our son, "Why?!" When we asked him this, Jacob usually responded with extreme internal anxiety, and we just become angry. I brought this revolutionary concept home with me after the conference and my husband and I purposefully started practicing new responses to Jacob. When Jacob misbehaved or overreacted, rather than just getting heated and asking him, "Why did you do/say/hit that", we addressed what happened by explaining the consequences and helping our son reach his own conclusions on he could respond differently next time. This truly took pressure off of Jacob and improved our relationship with him.

At the beginning of our journey with Jacob, I had no idea what a strong advocate I would have to become for our son at school. I knew full well that Jacob could exhaust his teachers, because he tired me out. He was also a healthy little boy and hardly ever missed a day of school, so his teachers spent a lot of time with him. Most of Jacob's teachers were amazingly talented, compassionate, and caring, but his constant emotional outbursts, annoying noises, and demand for attention could test the endurance of a Tendai monk. A few times, well-meaning people suggested to me that the best solution for Jacob was for me to teach him at home. Although I loved our son, I knew my limits of patience and decided this would not benefit our relationship in the end, nor enable me to retain my sanity.

As Jacob continued to frequently display emotional outbursts, have social conflicts with peers, and struggle academically at school into Second Grade, I started to seek outside help. First, I asked his social worker to refer us to a psychologist for psycho-educational assessment. She followed through on that and I eventually drove our son to an appointment with a nice young doctor in South Pasadena. After several hours with many breaks, her highly unhelpful, professional conclusion was, "Jacob displayed nothing out of the ordinary."

Next, I asked the school psychologist at Jacob's public elementary school to provide testing for Jacob. They said they did not do any testing until children were at least in the Third Grade. So, I waited until Third Grade, when the school psychologist, after assessments, determined Jacob was, "...responding normally to his life's experiences." Okay, again, not helpful. My stubbornness came in handy then. I kept asking. Fortunately, with a new school psychologist who was willing to observe Jacob in his classroom, it was determined that his attention deficit was greatly negatively impacting his ability to access his curriculum.

Yet, still, the district would not qualify Jacob for an Individual Education Program (IEP), or Special Education services, until I had him tested privately for Attention Deficit Disorder (ADD). School districts can be resistant to paying for costly services for students, but they also do not test for or diagnose ADD. Thus, I made an appointment with a private psychologist who worked out of the office of a local psychiatrist's office and paid $250 in 2004 for a test that took about 10 minutes. I was not allowed to join Jacob in the room for the test, but as I sat in the room next door to him, I could hear, "click, beep...click, beep, click, beep," etc. After about 10 minutes, the sounds stopped and the door opened. Little Jacob stepped out of the room, looked at me with profound exasperation and exclaimed, "Mom, that was sooo boring!"

Next, the psychologist turned to me in the hallway and remarked, "Those are the most abnormal results I have ever gotten from that test." In response, I thought to myself with a heavy dose of sarcasm and a fair amount of humor, "Oh, reeeally?!" My husband and I had the greatest laugh over that psychologist's comment.   We also felt relieved that a professional had finally validated what we already knew; Jacob had attention deficit issues. I was given papers to take back to his school so that the IEP process could begin.

The main reason that I was so adamant about getting Jacob diagnosed and qualified for Special Education services, was that he desperately needed some accommodations and modifications which would be legally established by an IEP document. For instance, in Second Grade, it took Jacob two hours every night with my help to finish his homework; that was not only cruel to him, but terribly wearing on our relationship. Jacob understood the basic concepts of the curriculum, but it took him excruciatingly long to finish anything. I knew with an IEP, that I could request shortened assignments. Instead of being asked to complete 20 math problems, he could do 10, as long as he was demonstrating mastery of the concepts.   Shortening nightly homework time took a lot of unnecessary pressure off of Jacob and improved our relationship.

Furthermore, I wanted to pursue an IEP for our son because I was concerned about how Jacob's teachers in future years might view and treat him. I wanted there to be legal documentation that he had some valid learning difficulties. I wanted to try to ensure that he would not only receive compassion, but also strategic teaching strategies to help him access his curriculum.

ADD was not the only thing impeding Jacob's achievement and social interactions at school and at home. I knew there were some deficits in processing along with his emotional immaturity. Yet, none of the testing, private or public, had provided any concrete answers. Looking back now, I can see that there were many signs that Jacob had a communication disorder due to his difficulty processing, receiving, and sending verbal information. He could have benefited from Speech and Language services at school.

Eventually, I ended up doing a little online research and came up with some of my own conclusions which helped us better understand why Jacob was the way he was both at school and at home. I read about Reactive Attachment Disorder (RAD) and went down the long checklist of symptoms and risk factors in childhood with Jacob in mind. I looked at a list compiled by Victoria A. Fitton, PhD, LMSW, at Michigan State University). Not all of the items on the checklist applied to Jacob, but there were enough that I had a true "Aha!" moment.

Some of Jacob's traits respective to RAD were the following:

- self-destructive
- manipulative
- argumentative (to the extreme)
- impulsive
- oppositional-defiant
- grandiose self-opinion
- persistent nonsense chatter or noises
- victim mentality
- learning disorders

Additionally, I realized that Jacob certainly met many of the early childhood risk criteria for RAD which included: young parents, observation of physical abuse/violence in the home, multiple caregivers, poverty, forced removal from mother, etc. No wonder Jacob felt so much inner turmoil and we were exhausted! Nonetheless, my husband and I loved Jacob; we committed to treating him as our own son and providing him with what he needed to thrive as long as he lived with us.

Dave and I also had the support of our extended family who accepted and loved Jacob from the first day he joined us. My mother-in-law, Dottie, who lived one town over from us, told me that she remembers wondering about Jacob's trouble with communicating. She learned from a social worker that our son was "language deprived", meaning that he had not been exposed to language/communication enough in his early years of childhood development. This can cause weaknesses in executive functioning which takes place in the frontal lobe of the brain and results in difficulties with sequencing, planning, problem-solving, attention, and memory (Sanzo 2019). Grandma McKissick also recalls earnestly trying to help Jacob with his homework on afternoons when she picked up our kids, and how he could forget something she had just taught him the previous day.

Additionally, my oldest brother, Brad, pastor of a church about 25 minutes from our home, would later also be a tremendous positive influence in Jacob's life during his teen years by including him on youth group trips and just accepting him.

Dave's brother, Uncle Bob, was fun and loving towards both of our children. Bob struggled with some of the same issues as Jacob, such as moodiness and attention deficit, so he had some true understanding; the two of them bonded from the start. Bob also had a keen sense of humor. One summer, my husband's parents, his sister's family, Uncle Bob, and our immediate family went on a week-long vacation trip to a collection of family owned cabins in the mountains of Colorado, near Estes Park, when our children were 13 years old. Bob took Jacob fishing for about six hours one day. Upon their return, Bob, ever the dramatic entertainer, jumped out of the car, ran over to me watching from our cabin's doorway, fell down on his knees on the rough gravel, and literally kissed my feet. He then looked up at me and proclaimed, "I thought you were exaggerating, but you weren't! Jacob argues about EVERYTHING and I mean EVERYTHING!"

Despite Jacob's challenges, we all enjoyed his strengths and were so glad he was a member of our family. For instance, he had an endless supply of energy and could be loads of fun. Our daughter finally had an imaginative playmate with whom she would create their live *Monster* video and puppet shows. Although Jacob loved to annoy Alisa and triumph over her in sports or games whenever possible, he was also fiercely loyal to her and depended on her. For example, while our daughter sold lemonade or peanut butter clusters at her roadside stands, Jacob would sell his least favorite Matchbox cars. My husband also had a son with whom he could build and shoot off rockets, sometimes with a hapless Barbie doll passenger attached. Jacob enjoyed joining Dave in flying remote control airplanes and playing countless video games. Moreover, I had another child to nurture, buy clothes and toys for, read Bible stories to, and kiss goodnight.

My husband has often referred to me as Jacob's "hero"; it was certainly not why I set out on the journey of foster care, but it was a result. Our son desperately needed a strong and caring adult who loved him, kept him safe, provided needed discipline, and stood up for him. I was happy to oblige. For instance, during his karate classes, Jacob would turn his head to the right and stare at me while kicking and punching in the air. I kept making hand motions for him to turn his eyes to the front and focus on the instructor. To my chagrin, he loved to tell bullies, "You better leave me alone, or I'm going to tell my mom!" On the other hand, he was also fiercely protective of me whenever we were out in public and incredibly attuned to my emotions.

Meanwhile, Jacob had consistent contact on the phone with his birth mother, Angelina, and younger siblings; he would eventually be the oldest of eight children, but the only one placed in foster care. Jacob's mother remained in Colorado and called him almost every week when he was first placed in our home. I was told by Jacob's social workers to monitor those phone calls closely, because they were concerned about the emotional impact on Jacob of some of the things his mom would say. For example, Angelina would tell six-year-old Jacob, "Mio, someday you will come back to live with us and take care of us; you are the man of the family now."

Jacob's mother also sent him birthday and Christmas gifts; huge boxes would arrive for him in the mail filled with clothes and toys. She even kindly included a gift for Alisa. One of Jacob's favorite gifts from his mother which he still proudly owns today, was "Mr. Blue Bunny", a giant, blue and white, stuffed animal bunny.

Jacob appeared happy to talk with his birth family but was moody after the phone calls were over. Jacob also had difficulty recognizing or talking about his feelings. I used to try to help him by placing him in front of his bathroom mirror and asking him how he looked (happy, sad, angry, etc.). He could not even explain to me how he felt when he was sick. It was as if there was a disconnect between his brain and his body.

Jacob's biological mother tried to earn back custody of him. Angelina showed up to his court dates every 5 months or so. Dave and I took Jacob to those appointments at the Edelman's Children's Court in Monterey Park, California. We were told to show up and wait outside our designated courtroom at 8 a.m. and wait (up to 4:30 p.m.) until we were called. The waiting time was also a chance for Jacob and his mother to visit. Even so, I had been instructed by his social workers to keep a close eye on Jacob, because his mom had previously tried to take him and run from the court. As a result, Dave and I never left Jacob and his birth mother alone but allowed them some space to play and talk within a few feet of us in the crowded waiting area filled with chairs and anxious people.

During one court day, we all took the elevator and went to lunch together in the austere brick building's cafeteria downstairs; Jacob's mother seemed surprised that we were going to pay for everyone's lunch and thanked us. Angelina was very young, beautiful, and expressive. For the most part, on these visits, she tended to ignore Dave, but was very open and talkative with me, treating me as if I was her teacher or social worker.

During the actual court sessions, fidgety little Jacob would sit in an adult-sized, black, overstuffed, swivel chair, far below the judge, with his birth mother on one side and his lawyer on the other. Dave, Alisa, and I sat quietly in old school, hardback, wooden theater style seats and watched the proceedings from the back of the courtroom. However, our identities and presence were acknowledged by the judge and sometimes he even addressed us directly. He would ask Jacob and his mother a few questions, then say that the case was being continued until the next court date. Finally, Jacob's mother would tearfully hug him goodbye and we would all go home.

It took two years before we could legally adopt Jacob; he was 8-1/2 years old. I know now that this is a pretty typical timeframe. However, Jacob had been in foster care for a total of four years, a long time for a child to lack permanency. Jacob could not really verbalize his feelings about the process, or so I thought. When our children were in First Grade, their teachers helped each of their students create a book with colored pictures and written phrases for Mother's Day. Every page started with,

"Mom, I love you because...", then the students either finished writing the sentence or dictated to the teacher. I was delighted to receive and read Alisa's gift to me. Then, I picked up Jacob's similar book for me and started making my way through it. I finally turned to the last page and read, "Mom, I love you because...you kept me." I thought maybe there should have been some kind of warning label; my mommy tears started pouring. Our handsome, energetic, argumentative, exhausting little boy was obviously dealing with some rooted emotional issues, although he could not generally talk about them. Jacob just knew for sure that he was loved and safe in our family. My husband has often remarked that Jacob can hit some real verbal home-runs.

The social workers and therapists at our private foster agency were highly involved and organized, but Jacob's county social worker (CSW), Joe, was not. He often forgot to file paperwork for Jacob's court dates on time, delaying the judge's decision on adoption. The CSW was also having difficulty finding and notifying Jacob's biological father of the upcoming possible adoption, a requirement under California law. His father had the right to object, but we never heard from him and Joe had to post a notice in local newspapers to show an attempt to make contact. The process became so mixed up that during one of Jacob's court dates, his judge apologized to us for the delays and fined the CSW for his negligence. He then ordered that Jacob be assigned a new CSW.

This got the adoption process moving in a timely manner. Jacob's newly assigned CSW, Mary, was both awkward and efficient. For example, one afternoon, I found a handwritten note from her on our front doorstep informing me of Jacob's birth dad's name, possible location, and that she had put a notice in the newspaper for him. I thought it odd that she would risk

63

Jacob's private information getting into a stranger's hands by just leaving it on our porch. She also liked to show-up for her monthly visits unannounced at 8 a.m. on the last Saturday of each month while we were still in our pajamas.

All in all, however, we were thankful that our replacement CSW got things done and Jacob's adoption day finally arrived on April 7, 2004! Dave, Jacob, Alisa and I, all excitedly got dressed up and drove 30 minutes to the courthouse. However, this time we were instructed to go to a different floor, labeled, "Adoption". The pervasive happy mood on that floor starkly contrasted to that of the oppressive feelings we had experienced on visitation days. On Jacob's adoption day, we were joined by our foster agency's social worker, Naseem, Grandpa and Grandma McKissick, my oldest brother, Brad, and his wife, Lisa, and our dear friends, Ken, Shelly and Alex Mikolasko. We anxiously waited for an hour for the tardy judge to arrive and later informed that he had been very sick but came anyway to not delay the process for us. The brief and formal ceremony finally took place. Dave's mom reminded me later that the judge kept repeating one phrase: "...with all the rights and privileges of a natural born child". She said it profoundly reminded her of God's adoption of those who seek Him and are given the rights and privileges of His own Son, Jesus.

Dave and I wrote a $500 check to the State of California at the end of the ceremony and ordered a new birth certificate for our son under the name, "Jacob David McKissick". He was now legally our son! We invited our friends and family to an adoption party the following month on a sunny Saturday at one of our favorite parks in Glendora, CA, to celebrate.

Raising our son to adulthood would not be easy. One night, when I was home alone, God brought me to my knees in a desperate plea for Jacob. With open palms lifted up, I told God,

"I give my son back to You, God. I know you love him more than I do and you have just loaned him to Dave and I for a brief time. Ultimately, he really belongs to you and I don't know what to do anymore. This is all I know to do." Our experience of "one step forward and two steps backward" with Jacob hold true.

Even after his official adoption, Jacob kept some contact with his biological family and finally met his birth father online one evening. I always supported Jacob having contact with them, because he was so old when we fostered and adopted him. I wanted the choice to be his. To this day, Jacob still has some phone interactions with his siblings and has gotten together with his uncle's family. I think that has been beneficial for him, because he has been able to maintain a connection with his family as well as see how many unfortunate circumstances he was saved from through adoption. In fact, the evening of the same day last November, when I met my biological sister for the first time, we traveled to Denver to spend time with Jacob's birth family. He even decided to stay with his bio mom for two days.

Jacob & Alisa

Jacob's Adoption Day

Baby Gracie

At our son's adoption celebration party in the park, we had a new foster baby, Gracie, an answer to my prayers. A few months earlier, I had been sitting on the floor, leaning against our bed, having a quiet time of prayer and reflecting on verses about God' incredible Grace towards us all. At that moment, I prayed aloud to God that if He would bless Dave and I with a baby to adopt, then I would name her "Gracie".

Dave and I had been waiting to hear from Serenity Foster Family Agency (FFA) about a possible placement. We asked for an infant because we thought that would be the easiest adjustment for our two older children. Moreover, my husband and I both simply adored babies and felt ready to take the plunge into foster care again.

The following week after that prayer in our bedroom, I received a phone call from Naseem, our original social worker at the FFA. She said that the agency had a baby girl they would like to place with us. I asked the baby's name and was told, "Her name is Gracie," the very same character of God and name that I had prayed about the week prior. After thanking God for His work in our family and setting up an appointment to pick-up our new foster daughter at the agency, Dave and I made a quick trip to Target to get equipped for a baby: bottles, formula, baby food, toys, a car seat, clothes, and foldable playpen.

Baby Gracie was a nine-month-old, beautiful, precious angel. She was almost always happy; her smile within her chubby cheeks nearly constant. Gracie's golden hair and bright blue eyes were a joy to behold. Once again, our lives were full due to a precious baby and we could not be happier.

Gracie's backstory was horrifying. Her biological father, more than twenty years older than her mother, lost patience with her one evening when she was two months old and crying. He picked his baby girl up and threw her across the room. He freely admitted this on a recorded video before a judge. Her parents took her to an emergency room that night where child protective services removed her from their home and placed her in foster care while her parents attended mandated child development and anger management classes. The immediate result of the abuse was that Baby Gracie had seizures; the long-term effects were yet unknown.

That poor little newborn who had experienced so much trauma was then further victimized by the befuddled child welfare system. We were actually the fourth foster home in her short nine months of life. Her first family spoke Spanish and her birth parents did not like that; they were granted a change of placement for their daughter. Her second family was not qualified to take a child with medical concerns, so Gracie was moved to another home. Her third foster parent was a retired single woman who was willing to take in two newborns at-a-time, but requested that babies be removed as soon as they could start crawling; she only wanted to care for newborns. That is when Gracie was placed with our family.

I was further shocked to discover that at nine months old, Gracie was still only being bottle fed. She gripped her bottle fiercely with a strength beyond her age. It took two days in our home before she trusted me enough to let go of the bottle while I was feeding her. Although there was a requirement that foster parents hold babies while giving them a bottle, my guess was that

Gracie's previous foster mother was busy with two infants at the same time; Gracie had to learn to hold the bottle herself, if she wanted to eat.

When I asked her last foster mother why Gracie was not eating table foods yet, she told me that the baby refused to eat anything else. Well, my stubbornness came in handy once again. Don't mess with a Mama Bear. There was no way a ninth month old baby was not going to eat solid foods under my watch.

That night, I took a tiny piece of cheese, stuck it inside the back corner of Gracie's mouth, rubbed it gently, and watched her swallow. Slightly fussy at first, Gracie's little blue eyes turned to me with surprise and her mouth opened for more; that was the beginning of her grand discovery of table food.

My husband and I tried having me stay home again as a full-time mom, so that I could devote all of my time and energy to be a wife and mother. I ended up going back to teaching after Gracie left us, however, because we ended up going into debt. At that time, foster parents were provided $650/month per child from the California State. This had to cover all of a foster child's needs. In Gracie's case, I needed to buy baby formula, diapers, clothing, bottles, two car seats, a stroller, a jumper, a stroller, toys, and on and on. The monthly checks, although helpful, did not nearly cover all our expenses. Nevertheless, I never regretted a single moment or cost of caring for any of our foster children because I was living out my purpose.

On the other hand, being a foster mother did feel lonely. Other moms were giving birth to their own children, enjoying baby showers, and having home cooked meals delivered. Dave and I were pretty much on our own. As I guess would be expected, no one threw me a baby shower or offered to help with meals. In fact, I was even asked once to provide a new mother at church with a meal just a few days after one of our foster newborns had arrived. I was happy to do it but thought it ironic.

One Sunday, a mother at church did tell me that she had bags of baby clothes she wanted to give me, but I never heard from her again. My point is not to feel sorry for myself; I survived. However, I would exhort people who know a person or family who is welcoming a new foster baby into their home, to reach out to them with both emotional and practical support; it will mean a lot. An even better gift for a foster parent/couple would be to offer to get Live Scan fingerprinted (the foster parents would get the form from their social worker or foster agency), at a mailing center, and provide periodic childcare to give them a much needed break. My mother-in-law did that for our family and I will be forever grateful.

All in all, Baby Gracie was an incredible joy for our family from her first day. My husband equally cared for her when he was not working, our children played with her, our daughter helped feed her, and Maggie, our gentle, red Dachshund, followed her around, licking her toes. Gracie truly was a roving ball of sunshine. Additionally, my parents, although in Arizona, welcomed her warmly, and my in-laws adored her as if she were their very own granddaughter.

Years later, during a recertification training with L.A. County DCFS, my husband and I listened to a social worker expound on the importance of developing attachment with foster children. Bonding, regardless of the age of the child or length of time spent in your home, is crucial for the emotional welfare of every child. At the time, I was thinking, "What is she talking about?! From the moment a child is in my arms and in my home, I bond with her; she is MY child as long as I am her mommy." I had no problems attaching; my big issue was emotionally DETACHING when a foster child left.

70

We thanked God that Gracie no longer experienced any seizures at nine months old and miraculously showed no negative symptoms of being thrown by her birth father. She could have experienced a long list of effects, including learning disabilities, blindness, brain injury, and permanent physical disabilities. I prayed there would continue to be no negative long-term impacts for her from being shaken and thrown. Nonetheless, because of Gracie's abuse, the FFA social workers were naturally on high alert and watched her biological parents closely. Despite her progress, there were still concerns and I was told to make an appointment to take her to the Cedar-Sinai Medical Center in Los Angeles. Gracie needed an Electroencephalogram (EEG), to record her brain patterns in order to determine for sure if she was still having seizures of any kind. My mother-in-law, Dottie, was kind enough to accompany us on the 45-minute drive and stayed through the awkward medical procedure.

Once in the exam room, I was told by the specialist to keep 11-month-old Gracie still and calm; how exactly is that possible when a baby is surrounded by strangers in a cold room and getting a lot of scary little things stuck all over her head? Gracie finally cried herself to sleep; it felt like we were there for hours, but, the entire process actually only took about 90 minutes. I really think her biological parents should have been mandated to attend that medical procedure; her father should have watched the results of his actions. Nonetheless, the test results were negative and Gracie no longer experienced seizures.

The FFA social workers then told Dave and I that Gracie's parents were complying with all the requirements from the state to get their daughter returned to them and that we would need to bring her for weekly visits to Serenity Foster Family Home. A few months later, the frequency of visits with her parents increased. All the while, we were subtly being given the message from the private social workers that they were hoping Mercy would be able to stay with our family, but that the official plan, as was usual, was reunification with her birth parents. This was probably the hardest part of being foster parents who desired to adopt. We were setting ourselves up for inevitable heartbreak; however, we knew we were also providing a tiny, helpless child everything she needed to thrive.

My husband was teaching full-time and our older two children were in school every day, so it was mostly up to me to transport Gracie to and from her family visitations. Considering my protective instinct and automatic love for Gracie, I discovered that I was unexpectedly faced with an intense, inner conflict. My immediate tendency whenever I saw Gracie's father was to scream at him, "Monster!" In my estimation, there was not a more heinous crime than harming a helpless child. I felt pity for her seemingly sweet mother, a much younger, very pretty woman with long blond hair who had herself grown up in the foster care system; she appeared intimidated by her older husband.

I had to find a way to deal with my feelings towards Gracie's dad; I was going to be seeing him often and felt convicted that I had to practice humility in order to be a positive Christian witness to the couple. I decided prayer was going to be the only weapon I had available in order to counter my natural tendencies. So, before every visit I asked God to fill me with HIS mercy for Gracie's parents, as everything human in me wanted to rebel. Through that exercise of discipline, God did answer my prayers and I was able to greet our foster baby's dad with gentleness in my actions that I did not feel.

Gracie's parents were always positive towards my husband and I, thanking us for caring for her. One morning, at our weekly drop off, her dad told me that we were "cool" Christians. I am not sure what he meant by that, but I assume he was saying that he felt safe with us (or maybe it was just the leopard print baby outfit I bought that he liked so much). Her parents also got tired of being monitored so closely by the FFA social workers at their visits and requested that they get moved to a private counseling office. It seemed to us that her parents got whatever they asked for; after that, I was dropping Gracie off at an impersonal office on the 5th floor of a bank building. Eventually, I would end up taking our foster daughter to a third location farther away for family therapy sessions where her parents received instruction in how to play and interact with their daughter. Meanwhile, Gracie's birth father who had thrown her across the room like a football when she was two months old, was also attending six months of mandated anger management classes.

Logically, I told myself that Gracie did not belong to our family and the plan was reunification with her biological parents; however, it was impossible for me to emotionally disengage from her. I loved our foster baby as if she was my own child. The drop-offs for visits with her parents were particularly difficult for me, because I helplessly felt like I was abandoning her.

One of my favorite movies is *Blindside*, a true story about NFL player, Michael Oher, who as a homeless teen was taken in by a caring family, the Tuohys. Not only do I relate to the spunky (and highly assertive), wife and mother in the movie, but I also love a particular scene in the movie in which Michael's high school football coach is "schooled" by the foster mother when she tells him, "You should really get to know your players. Michael scored in the ninety-eight percentile in protective instincts." Well, I am pretty sure Michael Oher and I share that trait. My greatest desire as a foster mom was to protect our foster baby, but of course, so much was out of my control.

Gracie blossomed in our home and experienced a lot of "firsts": her first time eating food, her first-time walking, her first time talking, and her first birthday party complete with *Hello Kitty* decorations and a living room floor covered with balloons to gleefully chase. At the end of her stay with us, by 16 months of age, Gracie was walking around the house imitating our older children doing homework, and calling me, "Mama". Thankfully, we did not notice any signs of brain damage or delays in her development and prayed this continued to be the case.

Finally, seven months after Baby Gracie joined our family, it came time to say goodbye. Her birth parents had met the judge's requirements and they were regaining permanent custody of their baby girl. My family knew that day was coming, but the CSW had not given us an exact date. I was home alone one morning, when I got the call from the CSW who said, "The baby's parents want to meet you at 1:00 p.m. in the Denny's parking lot in Glendora and take her home today."

I hurriedly phoned my husband who arranged to leave work early. Next, I called Jacob and Alisa's school to inform them of what was happening and ask if they would call our kids out of their classes, so that they could say goodbye to their foster sister. I then finished packing up all of Gracie's things, put her in her car seat, and Dave and I drove around the corner to our kids' elementary school. We met Jacob and Alisa on the lawn outside the school office. They both hugged their foster sister, but Jacob cried while Alisa remained stoic and then they both walked back to their classes.

Dave and I drove away from their school and about five minutes down the freeway to a Denny's Restaurant. Gracie's parents were smiling and excited as they greeted us. I handed our foster baby to her mother and she was put in their car seat. Her parents thanked us again, then said goodbye. My last vision of Gracie was her chubby little toddler legs happily pumping up and down in the car. Dave and I silently watched them drive away. This wrenching moment of losing Gracie was the worst day of my life and I could never eat at that specific Denny's again.

Letting go of Baby Gracie was hard on our entire family but devastating for me; I could not seem to stop crying for a long time after her departure. It helped to focus on my husband, our two children, our dog, church responsibilities, and return to my career in teaching. However, I was acutely grieving and felt pretty much alone. I had always been the one on whom others depended, not the one needing comfort.

There were some particularly low moments for me. One evening, after the kids had gone to bed, I was in our tiny bathroom and suddenly just slinked down the wall to the linoleum floor, sobbing; I started jabbing the plastic toilet paper holder that I had just removed into my thigh over and over again as hard as I could. After a minute of brokenness, I stopped, and silently cried out to God for relief. I also remember wondering if that was how some of my students felt when they harmed themselves, just desperately needing to feel a tangible sort of pain, rather than the debilitating invisible ones that I had been enduring for too long.

I did not realize how depressed I really was until about six months after Gracie left us. I was standing in our square little kitchen finishing up dinner preparations and our kids were sitting side by side on a little wicker bench at the kitchen table. We were talking about something that made me laugh and Jacob blurted out in a surprised tone, "Mom laughed!" Although Jacob often seemed very selfish, he could really tune into others' emotions at times. I was amazed by our son's comment that evening and it helped me recognize the depth of my despair as well as how it might be impacting our children. My road to emotional recovery began. The grieving process took time, but I simply made a conscious decision to stop dwelling on my sadness in order to be healthy and emotionally available for my husband and our children.

Of course, the rest of my family was also enduring Gracie's absence. One night, I was crying and looking through her baby photo album when my husband sat down with me on our bed. Gracie's lavender sunbonnet fell out onto the floor as I turned a page; Dave picked it up and started quietly crying along with me. I had never seen my husband cry before. I realize now that I probably should have asked our kids more at the time about how they were feeling throughout the process too. When I did finally ask them, Alisa told me that she had felt sadness, but did not talk about it. Jacob said he was somewhat sad but was mostly concerned about how I was doing.

Dave and I decided to take a break from foster care for a while. However, I had an interesting experience a few years later sharing with others about our time with Baby Gracie. My middle brother, Jeff, asked me to fly to Northern California to the church he pastored to share our foster and adoption stories on a "Right to Life" Sunday. So, one Sunday, I gave a ten-minute summary of our story. At the end of the service, I started walking down the aisle when a middle-aged, short-haired, blond woman approached me with tears in her eyes. The stranger reached out her hands to me and told me that she was a juvenile court judge and had to make difficult decisions impacting children's lives every day. I honestly do not remember what I said to her, but in our brief encounter, but do know we hugged then went our separate ways. The unexpected interaction with the judge challenged my assumptions. Previously, I viewed judges as unfeeling, impersonal and cold dispensers of decisions, but that woman helped me realize that this was not always the case.

Gracie's 1st Birthday with Grandma McKissick & Julie McKissick

Emotional Toll

I had little preparation for the acute emotional toll the foster care process would cost me. My husband and I also quickly discovered in the beginning stages of our journey that social workers (SWs) were certainly not going to be a source of emotional support, although they were the primary adults outside of ourselves who were the most familiar with our foster children and with whom we had the most frequent contact. Unfortunately, due to their heavy caseloads, our normal experience with SWs has been that they are frantically checking off the boxes of their "to do" lists. They seldom express any concern for how we as foster parents are coping. However, I am very pleased to be able to say that in the last few months with our current foster son, we have had the fortune to be working with three very caring SWs; rare indeed.

Nonetheless, my suggestion is that if American child welfare policy makers truly want to recruit and keep quality foster parents for our most marginalized children, then they should seek to provide some level of sensitivity and support training for social workers. Foster families desperately need assistance in positively weathering both the initial adjustment of receiving new foster children and the grieving process after they leave. Foster parents are people, not commodities; we are human beings with feelings, not robots. Sadly, I have commonly felt like an expendable means to an end in my interactions with social workers (especially those from the county), rather than a valuable team member working for the common good of our nation's helpless, abused, and neglected children.

Marianna

After Baby Gracie left, Dave and I eventually felt ready to welcome another foster child into our home. This time around, though, I would be teaching again and needed to find childcare. It did not take long before three-year-old Marianna, with her beautiful, curly, dark brown hair, chocolate eyes and spunky personality was placed into our home. Marianna was a middle child; she had a five-year-old brother and a one-year-old brother who lived in a different foster home. They had previously been placed together, but her misbehavior demonstrated to her social worker that she needed more attention than she was getting. In fact, Marianna had tried to hurt her baby brother several times; the social worker who called us said she thought Marianna might do better in a home with older children. She also informed us that Marianna's biological mother and father were in their twenties and had lost custody of three older children in San Diego County. Currently, she was fighting in court to get her three youngest children back.

Marianna ended up living with us for five months. In that time, we discovered that she was an incredibly smart and precocious three-year-old. To us, she seemed like a little old lady in a tiny child's body; her awareness of others and her surroundings was uncanny. Dave and I had great fun with her; she called him, "Mr. Daddy" and me, "Mommy". Marianna especially liked "packbacks" and being on the go; one of our fondest memories with her was at the petting zoo at the L.A. County Fair in Pomona, CA. Moreover, she liked to smile and laugh a lot and taught me some Mexican Spanish slang, like, "caca", "chonies", "mocos", and, "chi chis".

Regrettably, Marianna had a tiny mouth entirely filled with silver teeth from the fillings she had received. Many children in the foster care system have dental concerns due to lack of healthcare and possibly because some of their moms put them to bed with a bottle; the sugar from the milk or juice just sits on the gums all night and rots their vulnerable baby teeth. In our son's case, a dentist had decided to pull most of his baby teeth by the time we met him.

I enrolled Marianna in a local Christian preschool where she generally showed happiness about going and got along well with the other children. Conversely, when I picked her up one day, I was informed by the director that she had yelled across the playground at her teacher during playtime, "Mrs. Jones, you're a PIG!" Yes, she was precocious.

On the other hand, the grown-up three-year-old could sometimes be inconsolably morose. A few weeks after Marianna's arrival in our home, Dave and I took our whole family on a weekend vacation down to San Diego, CA, one of our favorite getaways. We stayed in a hotel Friday night and visited Balboa Park the next morning. Four of us had fun walking around and visiting the Natural History Museum and shady, animal-filled San Diego Zoo, but Marianna was grouchy and complained the entire trip. She never smiled even once. Maybe some kind of adverse memory was triggering Marianna's negative emotional response, but at age three, she was unable to explain it to us.

Although Marianna had a positive relationship with my husband and I, she had some conflict with our older children. For instance, she would follow Jacob around the house and tell him in a deep, creepy, very un-three-year-old like voice, "When I grow-up, I am going to come back here and kill you." We addressed her disturbing behavior, and Jacob and Alisa sort of laughed it off, but it did add stress to our family dynamics.

Eventually, I discovered a little more about the environmental circumstances which resulted in such bizarre behavior in three-year-old Marianna. Her Serenity FFA social worker told me that Brianna's biological mother had used her children in witchcraft ceremonies and that this had understandably resulted in fears and misbehavior. Marianna's response to feeling threatened was to fight back. In fact, we were informed that Marianna's mother was blaming the three-year-old for her children's removal from her custody, because Marianna had "tattled" on her mom to a social worker.

Her older five-year-old brother's coping strategy was to withdraw. One day, I got to interact with him for about 30 minutes during a long wait at the children's court. He was wandering around the waiting area aimlessly, making nonstop noises and movements. I sat down in a chair quietly next to a window near him and called his name. I then asked him if he would like to play the "I Spy" game: "I spy something red; I spy something green", then he would try to guess the object. He stopped everything, looked me straight in the eyes, and calmly sat down in the chair next to me to play.

Marianna's mother was also present that day at the courthouse during the grueling eight-hour wait in the open, cold, chair-filled space in front of the courtroom. She spent a total of 20 minutes hanging out with her three children, then sat down to watch television the rest of the day. I tried my best to entertain Marianna, but it was a very long day.

Dave and I took Marianna to visits with her parents and siblings both at the foster agency and in public which were told to always monitor. One sunny Sunday afternoon, her mom asked me to bring her to a local park for a family member's birthday party. I was happy to do it but was certainly the only adult keeping my eyes on our foster daughter.

Marianna's biological mother ended up losing her parental rights with her youngest three children. They were all adopted together by an older single mother who lived with her son, daughter in-law, and seven-year-old granddaughter. I missed Marianna, but was glad she could be permanently adopted with her brothers. Furthermore, I knew that over time, her hostile relationship with our son would not have been healthy for any of us.

I did ask to continue a relationship with Marianna though. One Saturday afternoon, a few weeks after she had left us, Alisa and I picked the 3-½ year old up to spend a few hours with her. However, it was not long before her new adoptive mother told us she wanted to discontinue our visits with her daughter; I am sure she felt we were some kind of threat to their budding relationship. Her new mother also told me that she was frustrated with me that Marianna always asked for dessert after she ate her dinner. I admit that was a habit she had developed in our home.

A short time later, the foster agency's therapist called me to tell me about the session she had just finished Marianna:

Therapist: *Marianna, you have already had several different mommies. Which lady do you most think of as your mommy?*

Marianna: *Julie Mommy.*

Therapist: *Why is Julie most like your mommy?*

Marianna: *Because Julie Mommy gave me baths and put lotion on me.*

I thanked the therapist for calling, then had a good cry after hanging up the telephone.

Miguel

Following Marianna was five-year-old Miguel who had been removed from his mother and placed in foster care due to her use of Amphetamines. Miguel appeared to be basically a happy, healthy, energetic, and handsome five-year-old Latino boy. However, there was a definite "honeymoon period" initially in our home. After about one month, things started to unravel; his behavior and emotional issues became more and more pronounced every day. He was testing out our family to see if he could feel safe.

One of our biggest concerns was how Miguel started acting towards our 11-year-old son, Jacob. Suddenly, the five-year-old appeared terrified to even be in the same room as his older foster brother. If Jacob was in a room in the house and Miguel wanted to enter that room, he would freeze at the doorway and just stare hard at him without saying anything. Dave or I would try to prompt Miguel to move himself into the room and ask him what was wrong, but he would not respond. Jacob, although often hyper and sometimes irritating, was usually kind and we did not think he was the actual cause of Miguel's change in behavior.

Additionally, there were also several major bedtime concerns. Jacob told us that Miguel was playing with his hands down his pants at bedtime every night. The two boys shared a bedroom with Jacob on the top bunk and Miguel on the bottom, so the behavior was difficult for our son with ADD to ignore. Jacob asked Miguel to stop, but he ignored him.

Moreover, after the rest of us went to bed and fell asleep, Miguel would climb up to Jacob's bed and bite him in the arm with enough force to break the skin and make him bleed. The five-year-old never apologized nor verbalized why he was biting Jacob. Obviously, this was all very upsetting for poor Jacob.

Furthermore, after we all went to bed, Miguel began loudly screaming for two tortuous hours every night. I tried to comfort him by sitting close to him, touching his arm, talking quietly, and reading him a story without success. Miguel would just smile at me with a gleam in his eye and continue screaming. I tried removing myself, thinking I was incentivizing his misbehavior with attention, but nothing worked.

My husband and I felt at a complete loss on what to do. Our family needed sleep; both of us had to get up early every day in order to get our kids off to school and ourselves to our teaching jobs. Of course, I explained what was happening to his Foster Family Agency (FFA) social worker and asked for suggestions, but she offered up ideas that I had already tried. When I asked her if I could move Miguel into the living room to sleep, I was told, "No; he has to have his own bed and sleep in a bedroom." Instead, the social worker told me to move our son Jacob into his sister's bedroom, so that Miguel could stay in Jacob's room alone.

Dave and I realized that Miguel had some underlying serious emotional trauma which no one had yet identified or treated, but our cries for help went unanswered. One night, when I felt fed-up, I decided to call Miguel's FFA social worker after work hours and leave a recording of his screaming for 20 minutes to let her hear what our family was going through every evening. I did not get any helpful results from that action, but I did get an impish satisfaction.

I started exerting more pressure on the FFA social worker to get some help for Miguel, a five-year-old with obvious emotional issues who was placed in our home without any preparation. I adamantly requested that our foster son receive a psychological assessment and therapy. It took a few weeks, but Miguel did start getting some counseling.

Finally, I got some revealing information from Miguel's 21-year-old sister over the telephone one evening. I wondered why his county social worker had not previously obtained this pertinent information, but passed it on to her afterwards. Miguel's sister was very open with me. She told me that their mother had been a wonderful, healthy mother to her and her 20-year old sister, but then everything went downhill when she met a new boyfriend who introduced her to Amphetamines. As a result, she was neglectful with her youngest child, Miguel.

Worst of all, Miguel's mother did not protect him from her disturbed boyfriend. During that phone conversation, Miguel's sister explained what she heard one night. Miguel was screaming in the bathroom where he was alone with his "stepdad" and the door was closed. None of the adults in the apartment did anything at all. His sister also said that she had considered becoming Miguel's guardian when he was removed from their mother, but that she was afraid her brother might harm her infant son.

During our five months fostering Miguel, I was only asked to take Miguel on one visit with his mother who lived near the City of Los Angeles in a halfway house for single mothers. We were about a 45-minute drive away from her and she did not have her own transportation to come our direction. The visit between Miguel and his mom, which I monitored, was positive overall. Nevertheless, I could certainly see the clear signs of meth's ravaging effects in his mother's eyes and jerky mannerisms.

Unfortunately, Miguel's negative behaviors in our home kept escalating. His older sister told me that she believed Miguel thought if he misbehaved with us, then he was going to either be able to return to his mom or to his sisters in Las Vegas. In fact, at one point, she had promised Miguel that he could come live with them at one point but had no real intention on following through.

My husband and I eventually discussed with each another one evening how we did not feel capable of continuing to foster Miguel; his behavior was wearing us all down. It was especially impactful on Jacob, due to our son's emotional immaturity and sensitivity. Thus, with a combination of resolve, a little sadness, and some guilt, I called the foster agency to ask the county social worker (CSW) to find a different foster family for afflicted little Miguel.

We knew we would have to wait a minimum requirement of two weeks for the CSW to find a new home for Miguel, but one day, she picked him up in order to drive him to a couple's home who had two much older teenage children. My last memory of Miguel is standing on the curb with Dave, saying goodbye to the five-year old through the worker's open rear car window as the car started to roll away while observing the little boy roughly and rapidly scratching his right arm up and down.

Baby Ali

After a two-year detour from our foster care path, Dave and I completed another comprehensive recertification process and an in-depth shopping spree. We then welcomed Ali, a four days old baby, into our home. She was an "emergency placement", meaning there were circumstances which child protective services deemed threatening to her safety to such an extent that she was removed from her mother without notice and with police escort. The county social worker who hurriedly dropped Ali off at our house at 5 p.m. one night, told us that she had been born with drugs in her bloodstream, so was quickly removed from her young mother at the hospital. Although Baby Ali was recovering from prenatal drug exposure, she did not display shaking or anxious crying. Our new foster baby was calm and easily comforted.

One of the common requirements for foster parents when a new child is placed in their home is to immediately conduct a physical check of the child's body and record any findings on a printed diagram. This might include such visible marks as bruises or scratches. Next, foster parents must make an appointment for the child with a doctor for a physical exam (and dental appointment for older children), within 30 days of placement. This might seem like plenty of time, but there can be a glitches. For instance, a foster parent has to find a pediatrician (and possibly a dentist), who accepts Medi-Cal health insurance. It seems to be easier now, but in the mid-90's, I was turned away from a lot of doctors' offices on the telephone, before I finally found one which was also a reasonable distance from our home.

Moreover, a doctor expects that someone will actually pay for the foster child's exam. Ideally, all foster children have Medi-Cal Health Insurance cards to pay for their medical visits, but that is simply not always the case. Sometimes there are gaps in a government run, impacted child welfare system. For instance, with our previous foster daughter, Mariana's county worker could not provide us with a Medi-Cal card for her, so I just ended up paying the $70 physical exam fee myself.

However, when Baby Ali also arrived without a medical insurance card, I decided to try an alternate response. I made the appointment for her and took her to the doctor's office early. After I arrived, I stood with my foster baby outside and called the foster family agency (FFA), which was about a 15-minute drive away. I told a social worker that I would like to take our newborn foster child (who had been prenatally drug exposed), to her required physical, however, I did not have her medical card. I went on to explain that our family could not afford to keep on paying for all of the visits ourselves and asked if she could please come bring me the $70 for the appointment. The social worker was not pleased with me, but she did it.

The money we spent on appointments was not the primary issue for me. What got under my skin was the disparity of expectations placed upon us, the foster parents, and the county social workers. Dave and I had a myriad of regulations we were directed to not only complete without question, but also within a regimented time frame. Conversely, we repeatedly witnessed the social service system fail our helpless foster children in countless ways and apparently without any accountability.

Baby Ali only lived with us for two months, so our attachment to her was not quite as pronounced as the others. Nevertheless, my "Mama Bear" protective instincts were still activated, and occasionally, I would roar. I can clearly remember the afternoon I met Ali's FFA social worker in the parking lot of a local drug rehabilitation residential facility for drug addicted mothers and their children. It was time to drop our foster baby off to her mom permanently. The young, naive social worker got out of her car to greet Ali and I, and with a wide grin loudly asked me, "Isn't this WONDERFUL?!"

I did not respond the way she expected me to, for I had been to the residence and met Ali's mother previously when I had taken her there for visits. At those drop-offs, I was asked to leave the newborn in her carrier, wait for a social worker (sw), and her mother to come get her, then walk out. During one such occasion, Ali's mother told me about the day she gave birth to her baby. The nineteen-year-old had been in labor at the hospital for several hours when she felt the strong urge for "a fix". So, she left the hospital, found someone she could buy cocaine from, took "a hit", then went back to the hospital to finish giving birth.

Therefore, when the animated sw asked if I was happy about leaving our defenseless, two-month-old foster baby at the drug rehab with her mother, I did not respond positively. I bluntly replied, "No, I really don't think this is WONDERFUL. This precious baby is leaving the love and safety of my family to go live in a facility filled with drug addicted mothers and their children. Ali's mother has only been in drug rehab one month! How can that be long enough to prove that she is an adequate mother?"

The social worker appeared shocked by my statement and the conversation ended abruptly. We then proceeded into the lobby of the facility where I said my final goodbye to Ali. I felt alone and completely powerless.

Baby Anna

Just a few short days later, my husband and I were asked to foster another newborn and emergency placement, four-day old Baby Anna. I was told that the Department of Children and Family Services (DCFS), had accidentally permitted the mother to take her sixth child home from the hospital. The older five children had all been previously removed from her due to neglect, including a filthy home environment. Anna was supposed to enter foster care immediately upon her birth. However, the nurses at the hospital were not informed of this important fact and a county social worker showed up at the mother's home four days later with a police officer.

After a brief and hectic phone call from Anna's CSW and only about 20 minutes to prepare, my family welcomed Anna into our home. Baby Anna was a beautiful, mostly content little baby and we all soon settled down. My husband and I discovered in our fostering adventures that it usually took our family about five weeks with a new foster child to settle into a regular routine and regain a feeling of normalcy again.

Of course, I expected to make an appointment for a physical for Anna, but for some reason, this time, I was told without explanation to take our foster baby all the way to a pediatric clinic at U.C.L.A. 's Medical Center. I was still working as a full-time teacher and managing our household, so driving all the way to U.C.L.A. was inconvenient. However, I did what I was asked and drove the 45 minutes in traffic with a newborn in her car seat in the back. Anna and I survived the trip just fine, but the doctor's visit appeared to be just like all the previous exams which had taken place only 10 minutes from our home.

We were requested to bring Anna to a visit with her biological parents just once. It took place at the DCFS office in Glendora close to our home, and I was asked to remain during the visit because the social worker was unsure if the parents were going to show up. I can honestly say that it was one of the most bizarre experiences I ever had as a foster mother. The county social worker and I attempted to make small talk while sitting about five feet away from the parents and Baby Anna. The thirty-something couple touched each other and giggled the entire hour; they showed more attention toward one another than their baby. The social worker and I silently communicated our confusion to one another with our eyes. Thankfully, the visit finally ended and I took Anna home.

On the other hand, one of my sweetest memories from foster care also took place with Anna. The county worker had originally told me a little of the baby's family history, including the fact that she had a sixteen-year-old sister who lived at the David and Margaret Home where I was teaching. Surprised, I asked for the sister's name and realized that she was one of my current students! I told the social worker this and one morning, Anna's big sister walked into my classroom with a bouquet of flowers for me and said, "Thank you for taking care of my little sister." I was deeply touched both by her gratitude and that I was a part of their relationship, even if only briefly.

Dave and I easily bonded with Baby Anna. One afternoon, just a few minutes after my husband had dropped our foster baby off at the FFA for a visit with her great aunt who was planning to adopt her, he received a phone call from the agency that four month old Anna could not be consoled; she refused to stop crying. Dave turned his car around and returned to the foster agency; as soon as Anna heard his voice, her crying ceased.

I logically believed that Anna being adopted by a family member was a very good thing, but my emotions were uncooperative. Her final drop-off at the foster agency was another of the hardest moments of my life. I simply had to hand Baby Anna over to her new mother, turn my back, and walk away with Dave, listening to her screaming as we exited through the doors of the foster agency.

Sisters - Jamie and Bailey

Dave and I were then asked if we would consider fostering two siblings, a 2-year-old little boy, Jamie, and his nine-month-old sister, Bailey, who were recently removed from their parents in the middle of a drug house in Los Angeles. We agreed and Dave got busy putting a bunk bed together in our son, Jacob's bedroom, so that Jamie could sleep on the bottom bed. Our daughter, Alisa, would share her bedroom with Baby Bailey, along with her crib and changing table, just like with the other foster babies.

Low and behold, when the two babies were dropped off that evening at our home, we found out that Jamie was a "she", not a "he". I guess the social worker either had not known that until she transported the children, or did not check the paper work closely before she spoke to us earlier on the phone. Foster care regulations forbid children of different genders or more than two children sharing a bedroom, so Dave scrambled once again to disassemble the bunk bed into two separate twin beds. We moved one bed into Alisa's room and the crib into our bedroom. As foster parents, my husband had lots of practice "rolling with the punches". Sometimes, there was also a lot the social workers were not told about a foster child or that was out of their control.

Our family of four adjusted to adding the two little girls suddenly becoming six. I continued to use the same childcare I had previously during the work week. I dropped off our older children at school first, then our babies at a little home with a big-hearted, petite Mexican American woman, an 8-minute drive away from our house.

Generally, I felt energetic and my husband was always very helpful, but I had also reached my early forties at that point. After feeding, rocking, and changing all of the foster babies we had recently cared for, the muscles in my back and shoulders were starting to protest. I suddenly felt tired. The best gift Dave gave me one night (and I highly suggest this for all new mothers), was to suggest that I take our daughter, Alisa, and go get a full night's sleep at a hotel nearby while he stayed home with our son and the babies. It was incredibly refreshing!

Jamie, the older two-year-old, was gorgeous, half Black and half White, and had dark, curly, kinky hair; I tried my best to manage it with detangler, rubber bands, and hair clips, but I was not a skilled stylist. She was also quite challenging. Jaime hardly ever sat still, liked to randomly bite people, loved the word, "NO!", and would laugh without ceasing whenever we gave her a timeout for her misbehavior. Another of her favorite "games" was throwing her tennis shoes at my head from her car seat in the back while I was driving her to daycare. Ultimately, I outsmarted the two-year-old by ditching her Velcro shoes for shoes with laces. She was extremely steamed with me when I triple-tied her shoelaces, but I was pretty proud of myself! Sadly, Jamie also start crying and screaming, "No! No! No!", whenever she saw a social worker's van pull-up in front of our home for a visit. We assumed that our foster daughter thought that she was going to be taken away from us and moved again.

Conversely, Jaime's baby sister, Bailey, was quiet and easily comforted. Unfortunately, she was also chronically sick. The poor infant had a runny nose and cough the entire four months she and her sister lived with us. I took her to a pediatrician several times and one emergency room visit in the middle of the night, but none of our interventions seemed to make a difference.

Jamie and Bailey's beautiful young mother was trying to get her little girls back, so I took them on regular weekly visits to the foster agency. I never met Jamie's father, but Bailey's father came to a few of her visits. The county's plan was reunification with the girls' mother, but she was addicted to drugs and having difficulty getting clean. Their social workers finally informed Dave and I that the sisters would probably be in foster care another two years before their mother could regain custody.

I appreciated getting an honest portrayal of the future, but it was also at this point that my emotions started to unravel. The foster care process was all getting to just be too much for me. Dave and I pictured our family, once again, becoming attached to Jaime and Bailey, to then just see them two years later return to their mother, where they would have about a 50-percent chance of living a stable life, wholly dependent upon their mother's ability to beat her drug habit. Dave and I talked, then decided we had to stop providing foster care for the time being; we recognized that I especially needed a break to recover.

We told the foster family agency about our decision and they found another foster family, a kind couple with a five-year-old little girl of their own. We then set-up an appointment for them to meet Jamie and Bailey at the foster agency. Dave and I packed up the sisters' things and brought them back to the foster agency on the designated day, so they could move to their new home. Predictably, I cried; I felt both guilty and relieved at the same time.

A few years later, I found out from one of the FFA social workers that Jamie and Bailey, as predicted, lived with the other foster family for two full years and then were returned to their biological mother. Unfortunately, after six months, the little girls were removed from their mother again and placed in yet another foster home because she relapsed into drug abuse. The traumatic cycle continued for the two little girls.

Breaking Point

Although Dave and I discontinued fostering for the time being, we did let our foster agency know that we were open to considering a baby girl for adoption, if they had one placed with them whose parents' rights had already been ended. We knew this would be an improbable scenario, but left that door open. A social worker actually called us within a few weeks and said they had two baby girls, both one year old and eligible for adoption, whom they wanted us to meet

The first infant who was presented to us was placed with a young, childless couple along with another unrelated baby girl the same age. My husband and I were provided very little information. However, we went ahead and called the couple to set-up a visit and drove to their home a short distance away a few days later.

The couple met us at the door and warmly welcomed us into their home. The young foster dad was holding a beautiful, content, quiet baby girl. His wife handed the other one-year old baby girl, the one the agency hoped we would adopt, with thick dark hair and beautiful eyes, to me.

Dave and I sat down on the couple's couch and could immediately tell something was seriously wrong with the baby that was in my arms. She was unable to focus her eyes on anything, moved her neck and head up, down, and around constantly, and emitted tiny bird-like squawking noises. I looked at the other couple and said, "Well, something is definitely "off" with this baby's health and neurology; her behavior is abnormal for an infant her age."

The sweet couple looked innocently at each other, then back at us and asked, "Do you think so? We thought so too, but we weren't sure." Dave and I thanked them, handed the baby back to the foster mother, and excused ourselves from their home.

We followed up the visit by calling the foster agency. I openly communicated our concerns about the baby girl they wanted us to consider adopting; I estimated that she was going to require a lifetime of care. The social worker automatically and defensively replied, "You can't say that; you don't know for sure something is wrong with her. She hasn't even had a pediatric exam yet. A clanging alarm bell rang sharply in my head.

I followed up with asking the social worker, "And WHY hasn't this baby had an exam yet? You told me that she has been in foster care an entire year. I have always been required to take each of our foster children to a doctor for a physical exam right away. Why is this child any different? Is it because you knew that it would be hard to find someone to adopt her if the baby was found to have delays?"

I knew I was being brutally honest, but I just did not care anymore. I was tired of the system and tired of my family being handed half-truths. The social worker ignored my question on the phone that day, but my husband and I moved on from pursuing an adoption with that baby girl. Fortunately, for the little baby, I was told later that a successful lawyer adopted her and then hired a full-time nanny.

A few weeks later, we received a second call from the foster agency asking us to come to their office to meet a different one year old baby girl; my husband and I hesitantly agreed. I had seen this foster baby on multiple visits to the agency with our other children and remembered her as a beautiful, golden-haired, but very quiet child who appeared to show little emotion.

The next Saturday morning, we sat down with a FFA social worker in one of the familiar side rooms of the foster agency to wait for the baby and her foster mother to arrive. We were informed that the baby's current foster parents were not interested in adopting and that the child's parents' rights had been severed. The social worker also told us that the little girl's grandmother and mother had been diagnosed with Bipolar Disorder, but that did not mean that the baby would have it too. That inner alarm started to clang again, but I also certainly knew by that point that most children in the foster care system had some level of physical, mental or emotional disability.

While we were chatting, the foster mother who had cared for our first beloved baby, Gracie, before she was transferred to our home, showed up unexpectedly in the doorway of the room we were in and with surprise in her voice, exclaimed, "Oh, hello! How funny that I would see you here today. I just ran into Gracie, her mother, and her two little brothers at Jack-in-the-Box in Covina! Mercy looks different; she is six years old now and has long brown hair. Her mother told me that she and her kids are living in a battered women's shelter."

I was unprepared for this unexpected update; my blood pressure suddenly spiked and I was unable to think rationally. The only fact that I could process was that our precious, royally spoiled Baby Gracie had left our safe, loving arms, to return upon court order to the same father who had thrown her across the room at two months old, only to face abuse once again. At the very least she had observed her mother being abused. I started to cry and looked helplessly at my husband, then told the social worker, "I'm done; I can't do this anymore." Dave and I walked out of the foster agency and I felt I had reached my breaking point.

I coped with my anger and grief by simply shifting my focus to other people and things in my life. It was a conscious decision. I was certainly busy enough caring for my husband and our two children, teaching, going back to school for my master's degree, and volunteering at church. I was convinced that my emotions would eventually abate.

However, that innate drive of mine to be a Mama Bear and nurturer would surge once again like tenacious Morning Glory that refuses to disappear. After another two-year break, I asked my patient husband if he would be willing to recertify for foster care again, but this time to have the goal of only fostering a school-age child and not hoping for adoption. I was ready to take on a different perspective. Dave and I were also teaching full-time and our two kids were now busy teenagers, but we had plenty of love and an extra bedroom to share.

Dave and I decided to recertify through L.A. County DCFS this time around, instead of our private agency, because we had a lot of practical experience already and hoped the process might be a little quicker. The first step, as always, was to attend a foster parent orientation meeting. Now, in retrospect, my husband and I like to refer to that experience as the, "Foster Parent Meeting from the Twilight Zone". I will attempt to describe it, but I suggest in order to gain a true flavor of that meaning, watching one of our favorite movies, *Instant Family (118:00),* starring Mark Wahlberg as a foster dad. It is a funny and fairly accurate portrayal of a couple who suddenly become foster parents.

Dave and I drove to a suburb of L.A. about 25 minutes away from our home that night and were warmly welcomed by a receptionist into the government social services building made of brick and metal window frames. After we received nametags and signed in, we were directed to the left, down a narrow hallway to a long, rectangular meeting room. We opened a grey, heavy door and saw two middle-aged women standing in front of the room, pictures of children's drawings and posters on the walls, and about 12 rows of metal folding chairs.

There ended up being about 75 potential foster parents in attendance at that meeting: men and women of all shapes, sizes, ages, and ethnicities. The women running the meeting introduced themselves as L.A. County Social Workers (CSWs), and presented a wide range of introductory topics, such as why children end up in the foster care system and some regulations for foster parents. People in attendance had some interesting questions. For instance, one woman raised her hand and asked, "If only 6 children are allowed in one foster home, what if I own six homes? Can I have 36 foster children?" I guess she saw gigantic dollar signs floating all around the room. Another lady raised her hand and randomly started sharing a story of horrendous abuse in a foster home that she had heard about in 1986, 25 years previous. When the CSWs reviewed what items need to be included in a foster home's first aid kit and how medical interventions needed to be recorded, a man questioned if foster parents needed to write down every time they used a band-aid.

My husband survived the two-hour experience; we were pretty used to jumping through the many hoops of requirements by then. We were willing to put up with them because the tedious means justified the end of providing care for a foster child. Some of the people attending the orientation that night, however, were first timers. In fact, as we were walking out of the meeting room, we were surprised by a young couple running after us who got our attention by saying, "Hi there! You two seem normal; can we ask you a few questions?" Dave and I were happy to chat, but that memory has forever been a source of humor for us.

After the orientation, Dave and I attended several all-day Saturday training sessions run by CSWs at Citrus Community College in Glendora, CA. We ended up making a strong connection with the other foster parents in our group which was a novel experience for us. We even hosted a monthly potluck dinner at our home for our group to stay in touch and support one another.

After finishing all of the requirements, my husband and I waited for a phone call for a possible placement. We had clearly stated several times that we were ready to foster one school-age child, since we were both working full-time. Jacob was also continuing to prove a challenge to parent and we did not want to take on more than we could handle by accepting multiple siblings. I got a phone call one afternoon from a L.A. County DCFS social worker who asked if we would consider fostering an infant. I replied politely, but firmly, "No; I'm sorry, but no."

The second phone call from DCFS a few weeks later was a request that we foster two sisters, ages one and three years old. I spoke with Dave, but answered, "I'm sorry, no. With our current lifestyle and our son's needs, we only feel comfortable taking one school-age child." We waited another two silent years and received no more phone calls; I checked in a few times with DCFS, but never got any answers.

Dave and I finally decided to move on once again. I could not fathom what the delay was in getting a placement; I knew there must have been at least one school-age foster child in L.A. County who needed a loving home. However, I concluded that God's plan for us must be different than our own. I then devoted myself whole-heartedly to our family and my students.

Reunification Policy

Undoubtedly, the experiences and losses we had in L.A. County's foster care system changed my outlook on people and life in general. I cannot imagine how it feels (although I did through the process with a good friend who battled mental illness), to be a parent whose children are forcibly removed from me. The reasons for removal vary greatly, but for those parents who truly love their children, I envision that their feelings of fear and loss of control must be overwhelming. I do believe that it is best for a child to be reunited with his/her biological parent(s), if the child's safety is assured. Conversely, I also think that a parent who has shown gross neglect or caused irreversible physical harm to a child should lose the privilege of parenthood.

Who makes the decision that biological parents are ready to have their children placed back in their homes and how did the policy of family reunification become the standard in the United States? Every organization, including the Los Angeles County's Department of Children and Family Services (DCFS), has a chain of command. The following is a basic list from my perspective (a foster/adoptive parent and teacher of teens from DCFS and the juvenile probation system for a span of 25 years), of those people wielding power over our vulnerable foster children with the most power at the top of the list to those with the least amount of power at the bottom:

1. Juvenile Court Judges
2. County Social Workers

3. Biological Parents
4. Children's Advocates/Lawyers
5. Private Foster Agency Social Workers
6. Children
7. Foster Parents

Juvenile court judges, those at the top of my power list, are also answerable to a force higher than themselves: written laws. Primarily focusing on reunification with birth parents for foster children is a legal mandate which began with the *Adoption Assistance and Child Welfare Act of 1980*. According to *Child and Family Services Reviews*, "The *Adoption Assistance and Child Welfare Act of 1980,* requires that child protective services (CPS), agencies make reasonable efforts to avoid unnecessary removal of children from their homes and to reunify foster children with their families whenever possible. "Reasonable efforts" means providing parents with useful resources that enable them to protect the child, provide a stable home environment, and promote the child's well-being" (The Adoption Assistance 2017).

There are quite a few glaringly vague adjectives and nouns used in the above sentence: "reasonable", "useful", "stable", and "well-being". Who measures these standards and makes these decisions? It is the states' judges who rely mostly on the advice and information provided to them by county social workers who almost always lean towards favoring reunification with biological families. Reunification, in fact, makes up at least 70 percent of the permanent outcomes for children placed in foster care in California. However, some of us who have firsthand, long term experience with the child welfare system, would say that this stringent focus on reunification with birth parents often tragically takes place at the cost of the very children who are supposed to be protected by these entities. The hard truth is that although foster parents are necessary resources in the care of children placed in child protective services, they have very little to no say in the final placement decisions made on behalf of their foster children (Lawson, et al. 2017).

Another more recent law, the *Family First Prevention Services Act*, was signed into effect in February 2018, and upended how states in America spend the $8 billion in federal funds they receive for the prevention of child abuse. The basic requirement of the law is that states now show proof that they are spending federal funds which focus on well-proven programs that provide early interventions for children at-risk of abuse and neglect in their families of origin, such as parenting classes and drug rehabilitation, so that children can avoid being removed from their parents altogether (Wiltz 2018). That law makes sense. Nonetheless, just like the fairytales I loved hearing as a little girl, real-life outcomes are often different from well-meaning intentions.

I have been "preaching" early intervention for at-risk children to my professional colleagues for years; I am not sure how anyone could really argue against it. At first glance, the *Family First Act* appears to potentially be amazingly beneficial for endangered children all over America, but read a little deeper and you will discover that its guidelines only allow monies for interventions to start after a child has already been identified as a potential foster care placement. This means that reports of severe neglect or abuse in the child's home of origin have already been documented. Therefore, in actuality, according to *Social Work Today* (2020), this law focuses more on, "...family preservation...", than on prevention of child abuse. Furthermore, another concern of child advocates is that this legislation eliminates stipends and services for extended family members who step in to be caregivers, such as grandparents. The FFPS Act also limits assistance to parents of children identified as being abused by them to a 12-month time span; many experts in the field do not think that is enough time to ensure that these parents are fully rehabilitated (Getz 2020).

Additionally, although there are some legal guidelines for spending federal funding in the U.S., individual states still have some leeway and can differ widely both in policies and outcomes regarding foster care. For instance, in 2016, there was an approximate total of 437,500 foster children in the United States. Virginia State had the lowest number of 4,890 children living in foster homes or group homes, because its child welfare system focuses more on adoption, rather than on reunification with parents. In fact, according to Jacques (2018), 60% of foster children in Virginia are eventually adopted by their foster parents. Conversely, New Jersey State reported 6,527 foster children in 2015 (with an impressive 91% of these kids placed in foster family homes, rather than in institutional settings), but only about 21.5% were adopted (NACAC 2014). In comparison, Jacques (2018) reported California State to have an estimated 54,685 foster children in 2016 (with one-third residing in Los Angeles County), and less than 9% of these children were adopted (Child Trends 2015). A common concern for child advocates in all states is a disturbing rise in the removal of children from their birth parents due to an increase in opioid addiction. This is combined along with an unfortunate shortage of Americans willing to become foster parents due to low stipends and poor chances of adopting their foster children (Jacques 2018).

Yo-Yos

The emotional fallout for children trapped in a cycle of perpetual removal from and reunification with their biological parents is devastating. These foster children can experience a lifetime of trauma, recurring trouble with law enforcement, and a continual disruption of their education. In my 20 years of teaching teens from Los Angeles County DCFS and juvenile probation, I was often heartbroken over seeing them being treated as if they were human yo-yos. The sad fact is that the average foster child in America will have three different placements while growing up; however, some can have up to 20-30 different homes (Facts on 2006).

Of course, if a child's home changes, then mostly likely so does his school. Approximately 33 percent of foster care children in the United States change elementary schools at least five times, putting them at greater risk of falling behind academically (Nfyiadmin 2017). Foster children end up losing about, "...four to six months of academic progress per move..." (Lahey 2014).

The current trend in California is to shorten children's length of stays in foster care as much as possible. In fact, in 2007, of those children who entered foster care, 54 percent of them left within one year. Yet does mandating shorter stays decrease or increase the trauma foster children experience? Even though this fairly recent idea of shorter stays in foster care may be well-intentioned, I have seen that it can further distress children due to additional adjustments demanded of them in terms of new caregivers, new schools, new teachers, and new friends,

Moreover, foster, probation or homeless children frequently have difficulty focusing on learning at school because they often feel caught in a survival mode. In other words, they are concentrating all their time and energy on meeting their basic needs of safety, shelter, food, and clothing. Love and affection come way down on their list of priorities. Sadly, many of these students are also the children who get in trouble and fail in school the most. According to the California Department of Education (CDE), in California State:

- 28% of foster youth are chronically absent from high school compared to 14% of non-foster youth.
- 15% of foster youth are suspended compared to 3% of non-foster youth.
- 56% percent of foster students graduate from high school within four years, compared to 85% of non-foster students (Foster Youth 2020).

In 2010, *AB216* was passed in California to mitigate the roadblocks faced by foster, probation and homeless youth in graduating from high school. Basically, this law ensures that any of these students who changed schools anytime after their Sophomore year of high school are exempted from the requirements of taking a 4th year of English and all Electives courses. Additionally, they are offered a 5th year of high school (if necessary), in order to graduate from high school (Assembly Bill 2013). Despite recent legislation, however, in 2013, WestEd, a "...nonpartisan, nonprofit research, development, and service agency...," published a report, "The Invisible Achievement Gap" (About Us 2020). It found that foster students, "...had the poorest academic performance, highest dropout rate and lowest high school graduation rate of any group attending public schools...," in California (Waters 2019).

In 2013, California also passed the *Local Control Funding Formula* which provides school districts in the state additional funding for special needs populations of students, including children in foster care. School districts are provided quite a bit of autonomy in how to spend the funds, but are mandated to create a Local Accountability Plan (LCAP), with the input of all stakeholders (community members, administrators, teachers, parents, and students), to clearly explain how funds are utilized.

As might be expected, some districts have demonstrated more intentional planning and programs geared towards at-risk youths than others. For instance, Bonita Unified School District (BUSD), where I taught for 5 years, serves students in both San Dimas, CA, and La Verne, CA, and has created new Foster Youth Liaison positions at specific school sites in order to support their foster, probation, and homeless youths (Waters 2019). This entails interceding with teachers and school administrators, tracking down previous school records, keeping everyone accountable for students' achievement and high school credits towards graduation, facilitating communication with group home staff, and being available for students to drop-in for conversations and cool downs when needed.

Fortunately, when I transitioned from teaching at a non-public school on the grounds of a large group home facility to nearby BUSD, I joined a team of people at Chaparral Continuation High School who showed genuine compassion for all of their struggling and credit deficient students; our team strove to provide both a quality education and an emotional support system. Our school was also backed by leadership at the district level who sought solutions to the increasing demands and needs of our foster, probation, and homeless youth. In fact, BUSD, although a quiet and relatively small bedroom community, about a 45-minute drive East of Los Angeles City, is responsible for providing education for the highest percentage of foster and probation youth in all of L.A. County, as compared with other school districts. This is due to the fact that when I joined the district in 2014, there were three large group homes within the geographic boundaries of the school district: David and Margaret Youth and Family Services (D&M), McKinley's Children's Center, and Hayne's Family of Programs (since then, D&M's residential program for foster and probation female youths has been shut down).

Strung Out Parents

How do children end up in dangerous, lifelong predicaments? One of the most malignant forces I have observed rip apart the childhoods of my students has been alcohol and drug abuse by one or both parents. It is an equal opportunity killer; its tentacles reach out to students from child protective services, probation, suburbia, and across all socio-economic levels and ethnicities. On the other hand, in recent years, I have noticed an increasing trend of students with single fathers in my classroom, due to mothers abandoning their families to pursue the destructive and deadly lifestyle of a drug addict.

Between 2000 and 2017, almost 1.2 million children in the United States were removed from their parents and placed in foster care because of parental drug abuse, especially Opioids (Yerby 2020). This problem has reached epidemic proportions. In 2017, in fact, 36% of American children placed in foster care was due to parental drug abuse with the top four states in worst shape being Wyoming, New York, South Dakota, and Wisconsin. On the other hand, some sources (Sepulveda & Williams 2020), show an unbelievably low estimate of 1% of children were removed from their homes due to drug use by parents in California that same year. Nonetheless, anyone advocating for foster children should be cautioned on blindly accepting such low statistics. Not only can cases of drug abuse easily go unreported, but the criteria for classifying a child's removal from a home as being caused by drug use are both confusing and unstandardized.

Sometimes public officials simply choose to misconstrue the facts (lie) for a myriad of reasons. What other explanation can be given when one source broadcasts that 36% of foster care placement cases in the United States in 2017 was a result of parents having substance abuse issues, while the *L.A. Times* (Riley 2019), proclaims that a report published by the Department of Health and Human Services and the Institute for Research on Poverty estimates that 80% is a more accurate statistic?

Parental neglect continues to be reported as the greatest enemy to our nation's children, however, social workers are left sludging through murky waters as they try to distinguish between pure neglect of children and the neglect which occurs as a result of the parent(s) abusing drugs. Parents caught up in addiction often also have disabling mental health impairments, irregular emotional regulation, the inability to respond to or meet their children's basic needs, poor spending habits, and/or absenteeism from the home for prolonged periods of time.

According to the Children's Bureau-Child Welfare (2014), the impacts on children of having parents who are addicts, besides the emotional trauma of being forcibly removed from their family, friends, and schools, can include one or more of the following:

- birth defects (from prenatal exposure)
- neurological damage (from prenatal exposure)
- impairments in cognitive, emotional, and social abilities
- attachment disorder (inability to form trusting and lasting relationships)
- anxiety
- high need to control their environments
- depression
- health issues

- physical problems
- greater likelihood of drug abuse for themselves

Approximately 8.7 million children in the United States live with at least one parent with a substance use disorder; these children are four times more likely than others to abuse drugs and/or alcohol themselves (Lipari and Struther 2017). It seems obvious that in order to stem the gaping, bleeding wound of the current status of countless hurting American families, our lawmakers, judges, social workers, and therapists need to focus more energy and funding on early intervention in the lives of children with parents struggling with substance abuse.

PART THREE
Teaching L.A.'s Lost Youth

Sarah

When I was a little girl, there were three make-believe scenarios that I would most often act out. I was either a mother, a teacher, or a preacher (like my daddy). Somehow, those desires continued into my adulthood.

In 1993, I was 24 years old and fresh out of the teacher training program at Cal Polytechnic University, Pomona; I had finished my Secondary Special Education Credential, but it was March and not the best time to find a new teaching position. I heard about a small non-public school, Joan Macy School (JMS), with 75 female students on the grounds of a girls' group home, David and Margaret Youth & Family Services (D&M), not far from my home in Glendora. I was told they needed volunteers to help students study for graduation exams; I signed up.

A few months later, the principal at JMS offered me a full-time teaching job but told me I had to go back to Cal Poly to get started on my Special Education Credential. I started classes again and began my journey in the classroom. I taught American History, English, P.E., and Health in Special Education classes for the middle and high school female students with Mild/Moderate learning disabilities living at D&M.

Our school receive new students almost daily because they were from DCFS and juvenile probation; their schooling was dependent upon their court dates. One day, 14-year-old Sarah joined my portable classroom. She was a wild child. Whenever Sarah did not get her way, she would run to the school office, throw herself on the floor, and start throwing a temper tantrum like a three-year-old.

Although temperamental, Sarah ended up being one of my favorite students; we even dressed up like one another one year for "Twin Day". For some reason, I tended to bond and work best with the most difficult students. I found my niche working with the D&M teens placed at D&M by DCFS or juvenile probation.

My student Sarah had lived with her mother for the first seven years of her life but was then handed over to her father who was a member of a violent white motorcycle gang. Sarah's dad apparently thought it was a good idea to keep her sedated with cough syrup. She had a rough childhood, got into some trouble, and eventually landed in placement.

When Sarah arrived at our school (actually for the second time; she had lived there at age 12 before I worked there), she was dealing with all of her family's drama as well as going through full blown puberty; that was quite a volatile combination for one girl. Fortunately, Sarah was a resilient fighter; she adapted, matured, and even developed a keen sense of humor. Eventually, she left us to return to her mom; I slipped her my phone number and asked her to stay in contact.

A few years later, after Sarah got her GED, she told me during one of our phone conversations that she had moved to Las Vegas, Nevada. She was trying to find work to support herself. It sounded like she was hanging onto life by a thin thread.

However, about five years after that, Sarah surprised us all one afternoon by travelling from Vegas and showing up at our school for a quick visit. I was relieved to see that she looked happy and healthy. Sarah proudly informed me that she was married to "...a great guy," had a four-year-old son who had

Autism and was a member of her son's Parent-Teacher Association (PTA). Occasionally, I was given a rare glimpse into the payoffs of all the investments we teachers had made in our struggling students.

While writing this book, I reflected on my time with my spirited student, Sarah and wondered how she was doing. I decided to message her on Facebook one evening in the Spring of 2020 and she called me back the very next day! What a delightful gift it was for me to reconnect with Sarah. We talked for about 1-½ hours. She was 41 years old, still lived in Vegas, and was doing fine. Sadly, her husband had died, but she was able to see her son graduate from high school the previous year.

Rosa

Rosa became my student shortly after Sarah and was a feisty, petite Latina who referred to herself as a "Chola", a "...hardcore Latina gangbanger from L.A. with thin, arched, angry looking tattooed-on eyebrows, dark red lip liner, Converse tennis shoes, a flannel shirt, and crunchy gelled hair" (Chola 2007). Unfortunately, Rosa, like many other foster children, joined a gang to seek a sense of belonging and safety that she was missing in her own family (Alvarez 2016). This choice, in turn, eventually landed her in trouble with law enforcement. Unfortunately, this is not uncommon. Abused children, in fact, are, "...11 times more likely (than their unabused peers) to be arrested and 2.7 times more likely to be arrested as adults" (National Council 2015).

No doubt about it, Rosa was tough to reach. She did her classwork but said very little and did not engage with others, including her teachers. I was dumbfounded one morning to observe an incredible metamorphosis in her. The Chola transformed into a princess. She walked into my classroom with her long dark brown hair curled and was wearing a flower-printed dress! Rosa resembled a sweet 11 or 12-year-old girl, rather than a hardened 15-year-old gang banger. I later learned that Rosa was trying to impress her mother who liked seeing her like that and had promised to visit her that day at the girls' home.

While Rosa anxiously waited for a phone call telling her that her mother had arrived, the rest of us went about our morning classroom routine. However, in the back of my mind, I kept waiting for the phone to ring.

A few hours later, it finally did ring and Rosa was escorted by my teacher's assistant to D&M's front office for the visit with her mother. Sadly, when Rosa excitedly arrived at the office to see her mom, her social worker regretfully informed her that her mom had just called to say that she was not coming after all.

The following morning, Rosa walked into my classroom as a Chola again. How did she feel giving her mom another chance to prove her love, only to be supremely let down again? Children, like Rosa, who have parents who chronically break their promises, eventually lose all trust in not only their parents but other adults as well; they tragically end up with a profound feeling of unimportance (Parentherald.com 2020).

Shana

The backgrounds of my students living at the David & Margaret girls' home varied greatly. Another twelve-year-old, a young Black lady, Shana, was placed at D&M because her mother had just died, and she had no other living adult relatives. She was enrolled in my U.S. History Class with 11th graders, because she was supposed to have Social Studies, but our school, Joan Macy (JMS), was small and we just did not have enough 6th Graders to form a separate class.

Yet, despite being much younger than all my other students, Shana was my brightest student and had the highest reading grade level that year. She also could not sit still, literally. A few days after she arrived, I just told her to go ahead and stand up at her desk if she wanted. Shana also had a radiant, beautiful smile; her joy was uncontainable, despite her losses.

Amazingly, I have been unexpectedly blessed to run into Shana several times over the years. The last time I saw her was at Walmart just a few years ago; she was in her thirties, had a successful career as an engineer, and was a single mother. Shana was with her eleven-year-old son who had a familiar luminescent smile and endless energy. After hugging one another, Shana introduced me to him and remarked, "I am concerned about his inattention in school; he just has too much energy!"

I paused, looked at Shana's son and then looked back at Shana. I laughingly reassured my grown up, successful student, "Your son is going to be fine, just like you."

Twins: Amara and Deirdre

One of the most disturbing stories I encountered in two decades of working with students from DCFS and probation involved twin sisters, Amara and Deirdre. They were fifteen-year old Latinas placed at D&M because someone had finally reported their mother to child protective services; The investigation was still on-going, but she was being accused of using her own two daughters to make money in her home by soliciting them for sex with strangers.

Not only was their mother's actions appalling, but she was also working in a group home for foster children at another private facility. I was informed that although there was evidence against the twins' mother, she would probably not face any legal repercussions for her horrendous abuse of her daughters because the girls adamantly refused to testify against their mom in court.

Any rational person hearing the twins' story might wonder why the teen girls were unwilling to speak out against their mother and put her behind bars. However, it is quite common for abused children to lie for their parents. Studies involving survivors of abuse have actually shown that the areas of their brains which control cognition and emotions are abnormally physically altered to such an extent that their attachment to abusive caregivers outweighs their pain (Sullivan 2010).

Ayah

Ayah was removed from her parents and placed by her county social worker at D&M due to neglect. She was a fair-skinned, sixteen-year-old young lady with dark brown, curly hair. Ayah had a diagnosis of Autism and was awkward both in her appearance and social skills. I later learned that children with Autism, like this student, are about twice as likely to enter the foster care system than others (Mandell 2018).

Ayah was enrolled in several of my classes, but I remember her the most from my interactions with her in P.E.; she absolutely loved to run. At the beginning of each class, while the other girls reluctantly walked and complained about exercising, Ayah would joyfully run until I told her she had to stop.

Ayah was also extremely bright. In fact, because she was so capable, she was finally transferred the next year from our non-public school to the local public high school. She then successfully graduated a year later.

After Ayah was enrolled at the public high school, I had the pleasure of seeing her again one day when I was escorting another student to the front office of D&M; she was waiting for her social worker to arrive. My previously dowdy student looked transformed. Her clothes were age appropriate and trendy, her haircut was cute, she had lost weight, and she happily answered my questions about how she was doing while giving me eye contact. I simply felt grateful to witness Ayah's butterfly-like metamorphosis: a result of her resilient spirit, dedicated group home staff members, and caring teachers.

Kara

A technique I quickly learned in my teaching of highly volatile and anxious teenagers was to give them space and time to adjust when they first arrived at our school. My students had usually been moved around way too many times and were frequently coming to us from emotionally and physically injurious circumstances. When new students sat down in my classroom, I kept a sharp eye on them, but simply went about my normal teaching routine in order to allow them to take in their surroundings and hopefully gain a tiny bit of trust in me. I also used that time to gather information, such as topics they responded to both positively and negatively, strong body language messages showing relaxation or uptightness, and ways my behavior was impacting them. After a few days, I casually start saying the new arrivals' names aloud and including them in classroom discussions.

This scenario played out similarly countless times in my classroom. However, Kara was one of my new students who was truly unique; I am sure I learned much more from her than she did from me. Kara chose to sit quietly in the front row of my classroom. I always gave students the choice of where to sit to grant them some type of power in their powerless lives, but if they abused that power then I would assign them a seat. Kara, although she could have chosen to sit anywhere in the classroom, chose a student desk which was situated directly in front of me. I moved around the room during the course of a class period, but during direct instruction had to be in front with the chalkboard back in the early 1990s. I assumed since Kara was in survival mode, placing herself near me somehow felt safer.

Initially, Kara rarely gave me eye contact because she doodled incessantly on her papers. However, whenever I asked Kara a "check for understanding" question, she always gave me an immediate and correct answer. It was clear that not only was Kara always paying attention, but she was also very bright. I decided to go ahead and give Kara her own set of markers and a journal to doodle in while in my class; if that helped her with her anxiety, then why not? I encouraged my co-workers to do the same when I heard some of them complain that Kara was, "...never paying attention," in their classes.

Due to privacy laws, our staff at the group home was usually provided very little information in terms of the reasons a student was placed at D&M. Inevitably, the students themselves would reveal quite a bit themselves to us. Kara, in fact, told me one day that she was in a foster placement because she was waiting for her court trial to start; she had been arrested for bashing another female student's head into the concrete back at her public high school. Although Kara was quiet and cooperative at our small school, she obviously had some built-up rage.

I discovered why Kara might be so angry one day when I met her guardians at her 30-day transition Special Education Individualized Education Program (IEP), meeting in our school office. Kara was there, along with her mother and grandmother. Her mother was smiling and showed interest in the proceedings, but she clearly also had a severe developmental disability; she responded to everything in a confused and childlike manner. Kara's grandmother did not seem to have cognitive challenges, but was elderly. It was obvious to me within a few minutes of the IEP meeting who was in charge and the "parent" in that home: Kara, the ninth grader.

It is easy to assume that children like Kara want to be in charge, but they really do not. What most children want, and need, are reliable adults on whom they can depend. In her fourteen years, Kara had only been able to depend on herself; not only that, but she had to take care of two guardians who were supposed to take care of her. The result was anger that she took out on everyone else around her.

Kara progressed well at our school for two months and then disappeared. Typically, I did not get the privilege of saying goodbye to my students who were on probation. Her social worker simply notified the group home staff that Kara had a trial date, the teen was transported to court early one morning, and then her judge made the determination that Kara should be placed in a juvenile hall in order to pay reparation for her brutal crime. I hoped that desperately needed therapeutic interventions were a part of that plan.

Tilly

Tilly was probably the most awkward student I ever had at Joan Macy School (JMS). She acted much younger than her 15 years of age, had a bad haircut, dressed like a ten-year-old, wore pants that hit above her ankles, often made strange and loud grunting noises, and had difficulty focusing on anything longer than five minutes. Due to these idiosyncrasies, other students were often highly annoyed by Tilly, making it difficult to make friends.

Nonetheless, Tilly flourished at our small school and found acceptance from her teachers. One semester, she was the only student in my Freshman Geography Class, so we got some quality 1:1 time together. She actually ended up staying at and graduating from JMS.

Tilly, unlike most of her classmates, did not live at D&M girls' home, but with her parents and two brothers in their home about a 15-minute drive away. Her public-school district was paying for her enrollment at our non-public school because they had exhausted every educational option for her due to her disruptive emotions and behaviors. Our specialty at JMS was providing a safe place to learn for middle school and high school female students who, for a wide variety of reasons, could not function back in their home district setting.

Tilly, along with her two (non-blood related) adopted brothers, had been adopted as a baby. Tilly's adoptive parents were older when they decided to pursue children and were already in their sixties by the time I was her teacher. Sometimes older parents and grandparents are more patient, but not in Tilly's parents' case. Tilly told us stories about how her dad would chase her with a golf club around the house, yelling. I was already concerned by signs of neglect, but our staff also discovered that the teen loved to get our attention by spinning outlandish tales.

Nevertheless, we spoke with both Tilly's social workers and parents about what she was saying and her physical appearance. We were informed that although the family lived in an upper middle class housing area and received monthly adoption payments from the government, the parents preferred to shop at Thrift Stores for the kids' clothing. There is nothing wrong with Thrift Stores, however, one of the requirements for foster parents is to buy brand new clothes for children in their care. After our urging that Tilly get clothing that better matched her age and size, thankfully, Tilly started proudly arriving at school every morning wearing up to date and attractive clothing.

One day a few years back, when she was 21 years old, I ran into Tilly at Von's. She was pushing the wheelchair of a friend she was helping. Tilly smiled at me, we hugged, and she shared a little of what was going on in her life. She said her parents had divorced. Following that, Tilly's adoptive mother felt overwhelmed parenting her alone and asked California's Department of Children and Family Services (DCFS), to find an adult group home for her daughter. Due to her level of disabilities and need for support, Tilly qualified for this kind of placement and was placed in a program in a home in a nice neighborhood nearby.

In California, parents can apply for the state to pay for an out-of-home placement for up to 18 months for a challenging adopted child with disabilities; after that deadline is reached, then the parents can apply for an extension as well. However, if awarded, the funding cannot be higher than the amount of the monthly payment for a child living in a foster care facility (Platt 2020). When my former student turned 21, she would be eligible to receive government assistance through the Social Security Income (SSI) program.

On one hand, I was disappointed for Tilly that she was not living with her family. On the other hand, I knew that some parents could reach a point of desperation when they felt as if they were drowning, especially those raising children with demanding special needs. Besides that, Tilly did appear happy. It seemed that living in an adult group home was perhaps the best option for her because not only was she able to be safe and receive the support she needed, but also attain some degree of independence. There are really many different housing options for adults with disabilities like Tilly. Regrettably, they are also often in short supply ("Housing" 2020).

Joseph

After our children were in First Grade and I returned back to teaching full-time, I spent one year as a Reading Specialist at Canyon View Non-Public School on the grounds of McKinley's Children's Center for boys, ages 5-18, in San Dimas, CA. There I discovered that boys placed in residential treatment were very different from girls. For example, males apparently primarily worked out their frustrations and anger physically. Examples of how this played out at school were such things as frequent flare-ups of fighting, running across the school's rooftop, or hanging like circus acrobats from walkway overhangs.

Regardless, I did enjoy working with the male students at Canyon View NPS. I called them out individually or in small groups to my office for reading intervention each day. More times than not, I would pick up a student from his classroom and escort him to my office. On one such occasion, I passed through the doorway of the 3rd Grade portable classroom to ask the teacher if I could take one of his students, when I noticed another little boy in the front row with his head down on his desk.

The teacher, seeing me pause and raise my eyebrows, pulled me to the side and quietly told me that the new student, Joseph, had been dropped off at the children's home the previous night by his foster parents. He had lived with them for over two years, but they wanted to move out of state and could not take him with them. The foster parents got tired of waiting for Joseph's social worker to find a new placement, so they simply dropped him off at the nearest group home and drove away.

I had heard and seen plenty of grievous actions towards children in my time teaching students within the child welfare system, but this was "a first" for me. I was shocked; poor little Joseph must have felt terribly scared and unimportant. I do not know the specifics of Joseph's case in terms of how long his foster parents had waited for the county social worker (CSW) to find him another foster home, but it is a requirement in California that foster parents give at least a 14-day notice in writing to the CSW when requesting removal of a foster child from their home ("14 Days" 2020). However, even if the CSW had been given the expected notice, 14 days is a tight timeline considering the shortage of foster parents in my area. L.A. County workers sometimes call 20-40 different foster homes for one child before finding an opening (Palta 2020).

Luis

After a brief teaching stint at Canyon View NPS, then returning to Joan Macy NPS for several years, I decided to apply at my local public-school district, Bonita Unified, in San Dimas and La Verne, CA. I landed a teaching position and at Chaparral Continuation High School where I met my student, Luis. He was a sharply dressed, short and petite Latino with neatly trimmed dark brown hair and brown eyes from the City of Los Angeles who was living at McKinley's Children's Center. He was enrolled in our school because he was credit deficient. He was also another one of my new students who unexpectantly chose to sit in a desk in the front row of my class. For two days, Luis, as if a life-size ice sculpture, just stared at me without any emotions until he began to thaw.

I will never forget the moment I asked Luis if I could help him with an assignment on his Chromebook computer at his desk. He nodded at me and it only took a few minutes before he started catching on. What shook my world that day was when he suddenly smiled, lit up like a brilliant Christmas tree, and joyfully exclaimed, "Damn, I'm doing technology; I feel so blessed!"

I was stunned and felt extremely grateful to witness Luis' joy at that moment. On the other hand, his strong reaction to something so basic made me wonder about the kinds of educational opportunities he had experienced before arriving on my school's doorsteps. Sadly, the poorest of our students from the inner city also received the poorest of educations.

Educational Equity

Childhood poverty is a flagrant problem across our entire nation, but disproportionately applies to children of color. An approximate 18% of all of America's children lived in poverty in 2019, but the percentage of Black and Hispanic children living in poverty was double that of non-Hispanic, White children. How do our states compare? In 2019, Utah, at 9.5%, had the lowest percentage of poor children, and Mississippi was the highest at 27.8% (Americashealthrankings.org). California's average percentage of kids under 18 years of age who were classified as poor in 2019 was nearly 20% (Daniels 2019), and a report published by Annie E. Casey Foundation showed that 25.3% of children who resided specifically in L.A. County were poor (Austin 2019). However, reported statistics can be grossly misleading, since there are far greater numbers of low-income households who are struggling to simply place three meals-a-day on the table for their children. In fact, in the Los Angeles Unified School District (LAUSD), at least 80% of the students qualify for free or reduced cost meals (Macias 2019).

Whether originally from L.A. or one of its suburbs, most of my students suffered prolonged poverty from the time they were in their mothers' wombs to age 18; quite a few had experienced homelessness. Poverty is a menacing monster in preventing equity in education for foster and probation youths. According to Alyn T. McCarty (2016), a lifetime of poverty can negatively impact children's education in the following ways:

1. Higher levels of learning disabilities.
2. Gaps in academic achievement starting in Kindergarten, ending with a full one-year gap by the age of 14 (when compared with their same-age-peers who did not grow up poor).
3. More teen mothers who often deliver babies with low birth weights which can indicate higher chances of future challenges in cognitive, physical, and emotional development.
4. Higher school dropout rates.
5. Greater levels of experiencing neglect and/or abuse.
6. Increased risk of health concerns: diabetes, asthma, vision, speech, immune system weaknesses, missing immunizations, and obesity due to malnutrition.
7. Mental health problems: ADHD, anxiety, mood disorders, poor impulse control, and behavior disorders.

Poverty is clearly a formidable foe for America's most vulnerable children in accessing their education. Furthermore, by the time these children reach high school, the impacts of poverty which result in gaps in their education when compared to the achievement of their peers have sometimes reached colossal proportions.

I discovered in my early years of teaching juveniles from the foster care and probation systems, that one of the most pronounced side effects of poverty they battled was anxiety. My students who displayed the worst behaviors were also the ones feeling crippling levels of inner anxiety. They had endured 15-18 years of chaos in their families of origin which was only magnified during the times they were placed in out-of-home care or juvenile detention facilities.

While appearing to be defiant delinquents on the surface, my students were really crying out for someone to bring order to their lives. I even had students openly tell me that they purposefully acted out at school or in their placements, such as punching a hole in a wall, so that they could return to juvenile hall where they knew what to expect every moment of each day.

I even had a female student one year who tried coping with her anxiety by copying pages and pages of a textbook down on paper; this obviously delayed her completing any assignments. Although she initially presented herself as an angry and noncompliant young lady, I eventually determined that she was probably suffering from high anxiety or even Obsessive Compulsive Disorder (OCD), and her attention to detail was her way of trying to gain inner control over her outside environment.

Almost always, if I provided what my struggling students craved, consistent order and unconditional love, then they felt safe enough to relax and engage in the curriculum. I created order in my classroom through visible lesson plans, clear behavior expectations, attainable social and academic goals, tangible rewards for acts of kindness and success, and consequences for infractions of school rules. The payoff for me was to witness my students enjoying the learning process and achieving, build positive relationships with my students, and have a classroom that was nearly free of disruptive misbehavior. I would encourage teachers who tend to see a high amount of negative behaviors or absenteeism from their classrooms to examine their own actions and attitudes first to identify possible triggers of anxiety for their students.

Many of my students' anxiety levels were also exacerbated by the lives they led in their foster/group homes before they came to us in the mornings or after they left us every afternoon. More than not, our foster and probation students arrived at school in a foul mood because of something that happened during the prior weekend on their home pass, or that morning at their foster or group home. It was almost impossible for many of these youths to transition automatically into the school day; sometimes we would need to give them adjustment time and personal space, an opportunity to speak with a school counselor, or a chance to take a walk with a teacher's assistant.

Unfortunately, too many of my students had not only moved schools excessively, but when they were in school, the quality of education they received had at times been mediocre at best. Understandably, students in juvenile halls often receive independent work in the form of packets or online curriculum. This can be a necessity because the students arrive randomly all year long, have a wide array of ability levels, and will not be staying long. However, students who are enrolled in non-public schools or public schools (including those like the continuation high school at which I taught), for any length of time, often receive boring packets or worksheets as well.

At Chaparral Continuation High School in San Dimas, CA, we teachers were expected to be credentialed and highly qualified, and provide California State Standards-Based lesson plans, just like the other two comprehensive high schools in the Bonita Unified School District. Moreover, our 10th to 12th grade students received direct instruction in all core and elective subjects, with the option of taking some online courses independently that were overseen by a teacher.

However, almost all my foster and probation students had difficulty adjusting to Chaparral's positive and academic school environment when they first arrived. Not only were they expected to interact and complete work in class to earn their credits towards graduation, but staff members smiled at them a lot; they were treated with both kindness and firm boundaries. Sometimes we would catch these students frowning and muttering something like, "I don't like this place; everyone is too nice."

In addition to providing order in my classroom, I found three main ingredients were the secrets to successfully teaching my students who had intense emotional and behavioral issues. Listed in order of importance, these were:

1. *Greet every new student warmly with respect and without prejudice.* Students who have experienced prolonged trauma and moved homes/schools a lot develop embedded coping mechanisms. One of their chief strategies is to immediately scope out their environments and its people to determine how they are going to respond to survive. Some will try to be invisible while others will be as obnoxious as possible. I could sense that my students were taking my measure within the first 2 seconds of meeting me; I did not have time to make thoughtless comments or mistakes. The respect and love I showed my students paid off too; it was frequently returned to me tenfold.

2. *Establish that I am the boss of my classroom.* My most difficult students had fun trying to take control of my classroom and could display some irritating habits, such as swearing, disrupting class, leaving trash on the carpet, and poking fun at others. I just let my students know very clearly on their first day with me and in preceding days

that although I would attempt to give them control and choices as much as possible, I was in charge of my classroom. Whenever they would challenge me on this point, I told them, "This is MY house; in MY house we follow MY rules. I am not discussing or arguing this point with you. You have the choice right now to follow those rules or leave." For the most part, I did not have to get to that point, because other students would frequently uphold and remind their delinquent peers of my classroom expectations for me.

3. *Provide meaningful, engaging, and differentiated lesson plans.* I have discovered that most students misbehave in a classroom because of one of three reasons:

A. Students are desperate for attention from adults and willing to try anything to get it whether it is positive or negative.

B. Students are experiencing an acute amount of internal stress due to feelings of inferiority or being overwhelmed in the classroom setting because of their long history of previous academic failure or fear of the unknown; they cannot initially talk about their anxiety openly with adults whom they do not trust yet, so they act out to purposefully get kicked out of the classroom in an attempt at avoidance.

C. Students are bored or they feel that the assignment is "dummied down"/beneath their skill levels.

Zaretta Hammond, author, describes this type of instruction as, "culturally responsive teaching" (CRT). Engaging our traditionally lowest performing students in interesting, challenging curriculum with which they can connect promotes brain cell development. Not only that, but when, "...the educator understands the importance of being in a relationship and having a social-emotional connection to the student...", it creates, "...a safe place for learning" (Hammond 2015).

On my first day as a 24-year old teacher, I started a routine of writing my lesson plans for the day on the board at the front of my classroom. I enjoyed planning and organization, but I also found that the first thing many of my traumatized students would do as soon as they walked in the door of my classroom at the beginning of a period, would be to ask me, "What are we doing today?" What they were really asking me was, "Am I safe here? Will I learn something interesting today? Is this important? Do you care about me enough to provide me with meaningful lessons? Do you think I am smart?" Eventually, after I repeatedly reminded my anxious students that the day's lesson was posted on the board, they would stop asking me.

Meaningful lessons are those based on state standards, diverse, require critical thinking and creativity, and have some type of real-life application. In other words, they are not printed packet worksheets. Students who have been shuffled around in the foster care and/or probation systems get extremely tired of being handed a set of papers and told to finish them by the end of the period. I observed this firsthand on multiple occasions in other teachers' classrooms while visiting other schools; it made me feel sick inside. Students in these types of classrooms not only feel bored with subpar curriculum, but also end up feeling devalued because the educators' expectations for them are ridiculously low.

Furthermore, many of my students who arrived with only a few credits towards graduation and failing grades were highly intelligent but had given up trying in school anymore. Often simple, tangible rewards like certificates (sometimes the first one they had ever earned in school), homework passes, candy, or gift cards were motivating. For others, just seeing their reading scores rise or a new pattern of "A" letter grades on their classwork was enough.

One day, during the 2018-19 school year, in my 11th Grade General Education English Class at Chaparral, I asked my students when some of them had "given up" on school. Two of my male students in the back row of my classroom quickly raised their hands. One Latino student from a local family in our neighborhood told me, "For me, it was in 4th Grade." By the way, he was also a student who constantly volunteered to read aloud in my class, a rarity. He also earned "Student of the Month" in my class that year. During his senior year, he wrote about how that award was one of the most important moments of his life so far.

My other student who raised his hand that same day in class said that he quit trying in school in 6th Grade. He was a young Black man in the foster care system from one of our group homes who had also gotten in some trouble with the law. Additionally, he achieved one of the highest scores on our standardized reading tests and consistently engaged in classroom activities.

I believe that children from disadvantaged backgrounds deserve more from educators, not less. California educators have a challenge, since it has the highest percentage of children living in poverty than any other state in our country. As I previously mentioned, more than 80% of children in the Los Angeles Unified School District live below the poverty line (Our Youth 2020). One responsibility of educators who desire to operate with integrity and genuine concern for students is to provide equity in school. This means that at-risk students, like those in foster care or with disabilities, are provided the levels of support necessary in order for them to achieve at similar levels to their same age, non-disadvantaged classmates, or at least to maximize their personal abilities. School can often be the one environment in which disadvantaged children of any age feel safe and valued; it is the one place they get to not only learn, but receive free food, have positive interactions with adult role models, and possibly achieve a fresh vision of themselves and their futures.

Unfortunately, too often, the most marginalized children in our nation do not receive from educators what they need to achieve and overcome all of the baggage they showed up to school with already on the first day of kindergarten, resulting in a lifetime of trying to catch up, and sometimes of just giving up.

According to EdSource, in the 2017-18 school year, "...only 23 percent of students in foster care (in California), met or exceeded the standards on the Smarter Balanced tests for English Language Arts administered to students in certain grades each spring, compared to 50 percent of all students statewide. In Math, only 14 percent of foster students met or exceeded the standards, compared to 36 percent of all students statewide" (Montero 2020). This poor academic achievement can eventually result in lower rates of high school graduation, career achievement or college attendance, and higher rates of unemployment and homelessness.

Sadly, research has shown that students who change schools more than once, are much less likely to finish high school than students who do not move schools. Foster students change schools once or twice every year on average, some many more times than that (Johnson 2019). One of the damaging side effects of changing schools is that children lose between four and six months of academic progress every time they move (Education Outcomes 2018). Only about 50% of foster youths graduate from high school and lower than 3% attain a college degree (Our Youth 2020). Furthermore, according to ifoster.org (2020), within four years of leaving the social services system as young adults, half of all foster youths are unemployed, 70% receive government assistance, and half experience homelessness; the result is a cost of $1 million to American taxpayers for every failed child.

I am now pursuing a career in educational administration, but previously taught both general education and special education students for the last two decades with a majority of my training and experience centered on foster, adoptive and probation students who received both General Education and Special Education services through an Individualized Education Plan (IEP). According to the Alliance for Children's Rights (Facts and Stats 2019), approximately half of all foster children in Los Angeles County have some type of learning disability and 87% of all children in the juvenile justice system have learning disabilities.

Fortunately, both the Federal and California State Governments have passed a great deal of legislation in the last 10 years to try to mitigate the negative impacts of trauma on the educational achievement of foster and probation youth. For instance, if a biological or adoptive parent cannot be reached by a school district to serve as a foster or probation student's Educational Rights Holder to attend IEP meetings and sign consent to IEP documents providing special education services, then the district can appoint a surrogate parent to do so. There are innumerable laws protecting children with disabilities that spell out the requirements school districts must follow to ensure equity in education (CFYETF 2019).

However, the ideal intentions of laws and how they are carried out in everyday life in America can conflict. I observed this time and time again as a case carrier of IEPs for my foster and probation students receiving special education services who had moved from bigger districts in California. Larger school districts in California, perhaps overwhelmed with high numbers of students and being understaffed, sometimes produce less than stellar educational special education services for our most vulnerable students.

Julie teaching at Chaparral Continuation High School in a Wonder Woman costume

Developmental Disabilities

In 2006, 47% of foster children in America had at least one Developmental Disability (DD). Identifying the causes of these disabilities is a complicated process. Did the child's traumatic life events, such as prenatal drug or alcohol exposure, being shaken, malnutrition, or emotional abuse result in a disability?

Conversely, was the disability present at birth and then did it increase a parents' stress levels and overwhelm possibly already fragile coping mechanisms? The strain parents of children with cognitive delays are under can be intense. It can impact not only how they interact with their children, but almost every aspect of their lives (Feizi et al. 2014).

What we can say with confidence is that children with disabilities, just like their nondisabled peers, have a much greater chance at thriving when they reside within a nurturing and stable family setting. Sadly, in 2016, American foster children, "...with disabilities were 2.47 times more likely to be living in an institution (rather than in a foster family setting), than youth without disabilities" (Cinahl 2016).

Intellectual Disabilities (IDs), is a narrower category within the broader category of Developmental Disorders. According to Elizabeth Lightfoot, PhD, MSW, and a professor at the University of Minnesota School of Social Work, an ID is a restriction in a person's adaptive behavior, or, "...the collection of conceptual, social, and practical skills that are learned and performed by people in their everyday lives". The abilities of foster children with an ID can also vary greatly according to the intensity of their disability, but most will require extensive attention such as special education, medical needs, mental health concerns, learning self-advocacy, and developing self-care skills (personal hygiene, counting money, finding transportation, getting a job, etc.).

The considerable needs of a foster child with an ID makes placing them with a patient and knowledgeable foster family extremely crucial. However, there is a shortage in the U.S. of foster families either trained or willing to take children with disabilities. Additionally, these children are frequently last minute, unexpected, and emergency placements; social workers do not always have the luxury of making sure they place them in a family prepared to take a child with special needs or might not have been provided key information themselves about the child, such as behavior issues or the extent of the child's intellectual disability. Grievously, it is the already helpless, scared, and challenged foster child who then pays the price, because it is very likely the new foster parents will quickly request a change of placement due to feeling overwhelmed or underprepared for the child's needs (Coyle 2014).

Leah

Four years ago, I spent one year as the Pre-K and Elementary Special Education Coordinator for the Pasadena Unified School District (PUSD). Part of my responsibilities was to organize intakes; I would decide in which school to place a new preschool or elementary age student enrolling in the district who already had an Individual Education Program (IEP). This also included foster students in group homes within the geographical boundaries of PUSD. This process generally involved me carefully reading every line of the student's IEP to determine which school setting would most closely match the services and educational setting the child's IEP team had agreed upon in the last annual IEP meeting. Additionally, I would scan a map of the school district to try to place a student as closely as possible to his/her foster or group home.

It sounds fairly straight forward and logical, nonetheless, the main issue that would arise is that the IEP documents provided to us from other districts were often out of date or incomplete, so I did not always have all of the necessary information to make an educated decision. Moreover, foster children have the right to attend school immediately, and so there is little time to seek additional information. For instance, one student I received from out-of-state, had a 3-year-old IEP (a new IEP with fresh goals is supposed to be created each year and assessments are to be completed every three years). His document was so antiquated, the entire 30-page report was entirely handwritten. Most of the time, however, the major problem in my role of deciding school placements was that I did not have the benefit of key information about a student, such as levels of progress on goals, prior behavior issues and recent trauma. In other words, I was working with a "skeleton" of a document with little substance.

This was the case with nine-year old Leah, who had Down Syndrome, a genetic disorder in which a person is born with an extra chromosome (Facts about 2019). Little Leah was one of the most heart wrenching situations I have encountered in my 20-year teaching career. I read her IEP and it revealed that she was living in a local group home, had Down Syndrome, and the special education services she should be getting in a regular public-school setting. I enrolled Leah in an elementary school in PUSD which had a classroom for students with severe disabilities who could also mainstream into general education classes with support as deemed appropriate on a case-by-case basis. I followed up the decision with a quick phone call informing the principal and then hoped for the best.

Leah started in her new school the following day. It was not long before I received a frantic phone call from the principal telling me that her school was not an appropriate setting for the little girl and that something needed to happen immediately. I asked her to describe what was going on and the administrator said that the nine-year old had had a very rough day. She had been screaming, biting, hitting, and banging her head on her desk so much that her nose was bleeding. The concerned principal had eventually called Leah's group home staff and asked them to take the child back to their residential facility for her own safety. I thanked the principal and told her I would work on it immediately.

After speaking to the assistant director of Leah's group home, I found out that Leah was naturally reacting to recently being forcibly removed from her grandmother's home. The young child with Down Syndrome had never lived anywhere else; her grandmother was the only caretaker she had ever known, but she had been recently having difficulty taking care of Leah due to serious health problems. I was fully aware that this kind of traumatic event was difficult for any child to deal with, but for a child with an ID, it was only harder. I imagined that Leah felt incredibly afraid and as if her whole world was spinning out of control.

Leah's IEP did not designate that she be placed in a Non-public school (NPS), but due to the urgency of concerns for her safety and the safety of others, I arranged an emergency IEP meeting right away with the staff at the non-public school located on the grounds of Leah's group home, so that we could change her educational setting. The confused child would end up still exhibiting the same behaviors at the NPS, but then she was at least in a classroom with a much smaller number of students, one special education teacher, and two teacher's assistants.

I felt profoundly sad for Leah and I had never even met her because the children normally did not attend IEP meetings. I did what I could for her by changing her school placement, ordering a special supportive chair, and mailing her a giant stuffed elephant in the hopes that she would hold it instead of banging her face on her hard school desk (she refused to wear a protective helmet). All the while, I was wondering if there was anything that could have been done sooner to help Leah and her grandmother with their needs, so that they could have stayed together. Barring that, it was too bad that her county social worker had not been able to find a foster home willing and able to accept her.

Mario

I taught a total of 15 years at Joan Macy Non-Public School in La Verne, CA, which would eventually encounter a severe decline in enrollment due to new legislation across the country from 2008-15. These laws were enacted to protect the educational rights of students in unstable circumstances like foster care and probation. One such law, California Ed Code 56040.1, requires that all students must be placed in the Least Restrictive Environment (LRE), to meet their educational needs (California Code 2020). For us at JMS, it meant that just because a foster or probation youth was placed at David & Margaret Youth and Family Services, our residential facility, she was no longer automatically enrolled at our school. After that, the residents of D&M were then most typically enrolled in local public schools; the exceptions were those who already had an Individual Education Program (IEP), with a qualification for Special Education services under Emotional Disturbance (ED). The effect of this transition was that our NPS only had about 25 remaining students who were all previously diagnosed with Emotional Disturbance.

After persevering in that challenging teaching environment for eight more years, in 2014, I decided I needed a change and applied for a teaching position in the public-school district nearby, Bonita Unified School District (BUSD). I was hired to teach 10th Grade English and World History at their Chaparral and Vista High School. The school serves both students from local families in San Dimas and La Verne, CA, and those from DCFS and juvenile probation across Los Angeles County (a majority who have families residing in the inner city of Los Angeles). When I began at Chaparral, these latter students resided in three separate, large group homes within our district's geographical boundaries: David & Margaret Youth and Family Services, Hayne's Family of Programs, and McKinley's Children's Center (however, as I mentioned earlier, D&M's program for teen girls was shut down by the state in 2019). Youths were placed in one of these facilities either by an L.A. County social worker from the Department of Child and Family Services (DCFS), or a probation officer from Juvenile Probation (Waters 2019). Students were enrolled at our continuation high school rather than one of the district's two comprehensive high schools if they were behind in their credits for graduation. Many foster and probation youth needed to attend our school because their education (and therefore their ability to earn credits), had been interrupted countless times by multiple moves.

Mario was one of my first students at Chaparral High School and was a general education student; he did not have an IEP. He lived at Haynes, a large group home for boys, ages 5-18, and had just been released from juvenile hall. The sixteen-year old, a handsome, Latino gangbanger with a shaved head and hazel eyes, was 6' 4" tall and built with muscles toned for self-preservation. When Mario arrived and all the days to follow, he chose to sit in the back of my classroom, as far away from me as possible. During his first two days, he said very little, but carefully observed the classroom environment, getting the lay of the land; although he did complete my assignments.

After Mario decided my classroom of 20 students was safe enough, he started to show his true colors. That aloof gangster became a peer leader in my classroom. I discovered he enjoyed literature and reading aloud, and he also often engaged in class discussion. He had a ready smile and was generally liked by other students, but did quickly let any new guy know who was the top of the social hierarchy of my students. Moreover, Mario had a developed sense of humor and gifted me his respect through eye contact and following my directions without argument.

Mario attended JMS and successfully earned credits towards graduation for about 6 months, until his probation officer recommended to his judge that he had fulfilled the terms of his release and should return to his home in L.A. Most of our foster students remained between 6 months to two years (or less if they went AWOL/ran away), whereas probation kids only stayed between 3-6 months. Sometimes we knew ahead of time that one of these students was departing and got to have some closure in saying goodbye. Other times, students would just disappear, and we would never see or hear from them again.

Mario knew he was going back home to South L.A. One afternoon at 1:30 p.m. I walked the kids out of my classroom at the end of school when the bell rang. Mario paused outside my classroom door, looked down at me, and quietly asked, "Miss, can I have a hug?" I smiled up at the gentle giant and gave him a hug, telling him to take care of himself and prayed he would stay out of trouble back home.

One month later, a female student of mine (Mario was popular with the ladies), was looking at her cell phone during a passing period between classes when she glanced up at me and commented, "Mrs. McKissick, Mario is back in juvenile hall." Although I was disappointed for Mario, I was not really surprised. Too many of my students returned right back to the same family, friends, neighborhood, and/or gangs where they got in trouble in the first place; why would anyone be surprised when they repeated their crimes? The merry-go-round ride simply continued for them, only being interrupted when they arrested yet another time.

Sex Trafficking

The transaction I observed only lasted less than 60 seconds but will forever be vividly imprinted upon my mind. One afternoon in the summer of 2019, I was driving into the black iron front gates of D&M girls' home to drop off some paperwork for our foster parent recertification, when out of the driver's side window of my silver Chevy Impala, I spied a beautiful Latina teenager with long, shiny black hair, wearing jeans and a sweatshirt, and carrying a backpack, pacing back and forth. She appeared agitated and was holding a cell phone in her right hand. My car was in motion and I did not have much time, but I still noticed a split second later a man in his forties sitting in a shiny black Mercedes parked on the passenger side of my car who was staring at the girl out his passenger side window.

Another second passed and I glanced in my rearview mirror to witness the teen girl getting in the man's car and then the car driving out the gates. I immediately stopped and flagged down an employee walking by and told him, "I think you just lost one of your girls; she was picked up by a man in a black car that just drove out of your gate back there."

The man replied, "How do you know that it was one of our girls?" I thought it was obvious why I would assume the teen was a resident at D&M who just got picked up by her pimp and chose not to respond to his question; I drove on to my appointment. I was aware that this kind of thing happened too often, but I had never seen it boldly take place right before my eyes in broad daylight.

The stark reality is that sex trafficking brings in about $150 billion every year around the world (Tiano 2020). In the United States, there are an estimated 244,000 children at risk of sexual exploitation, many who are picked up off the streets after they run away from abusive home situations. Girls and boys are nearly equal in their percentages of those coerced into prostitution (CPPS 2013). Most of these misused children are nonwhites, with Blacks being the largest exploited ethnic group (Nelson-Butler 2015). Furthermore, Los Angeles County has been named as one of the top centers for sexual exploitation of female and male minors (Human Trafficking 2020). San Diego, CA, and San Francisco, CA are also on the list of the top 13 areas for the concentration of sex trafficking (Shevlin 2016). Create Now (2020), reports that, "The average age of entry into prostitution (in the United States), is 12-years-old and the average life expectancy for these children following entry is only seven years."

Additionally, according to a report published by L.A. County in 2018, 85% of the reported cases of commercially sexually exploited children also have a prior history of being referred to child protective services (CSEC 2018). Tragically, many of my female students had ended up in foster care or locked up in a juvenile hall due to their involvement in this profitable and perverse industry. Despite being victims, these young ladies, some as young as 10 years old, were most often treated like criminals.

Thankfully, in the last 5-6 years in L.A. County, this stigma placed upon traumatized children has been changing. In fact, a new First Responder Protocol (FRP), was enacted in 2014, to assist law enforcement officers who are roaming the streets to find and offer avenues of assistance to children trapped in prostitution (Tiano 2020). Now, many police officers driving busy

170

hotbed roads such as Holt Ave., in Pomona, CA, just three miles from my home and sleepy bedroom community of La Verne, more often use words like "rescue", instead of "arrest" when detaining these teens (Day 2019).

Lamentably, despite the efforts of many social workers and police officers, children living in deplorable living situations still become runaways and see the offers by pimps of a roof over their heads, food, nice clothes, jewelry, cell phones, cash, and drugs as too hard to resist. Furthermore, group homes for children in the welfare system are often seen as easy targets and used by sex traffickers as prime recruiting sources for new sex workers. Residents within these residential facilities who have prior sex trafficking experience are also contacted to recruit other girls and boys living with them (Farmer 2017). Sadly, I heard about this networking system from my own students too many times.

Lashanda

Lashanda was a strong, gorgeous, 5' 11", full-framed, 18-year-old, young Black lady with a smile and personality that lit up my classroom the moment she entered it. She was loud and proud of her academic abilities, enjoyed school, and was eager to graduate. She was living at D&M and attending JMS non-public school (before the laws placing foster/probation kids in public schools), because her social worker wanted to get her away from L.A. and the people there who had enticed her into the sex trade.

I only knew Lashanda for a few months, but she left a strong impression on me. We had a mutual appreciation for each other and laughed together a lot. Lashanda had few credits to finish and successfully graduated from our high school on time; quite an amazing feat for a youth who had gone through so much. However, after graduation, Lashanda had a big choice to make; where would she live? Would she return to her source of problems, the City of L.A.? She could not stay at the residential placement and would have to find some kind of transitional housing for young adults leaving the child welfare system. Her grandmother in San Bernardino, CA, about 20 minutes east of us and 90 minutes east of inner-city L.A., told Lashanda she could come live with her too. I urged my student to take her grandmother up on that offer.

However, Lashanda decided against moving to her grandma's home. Instead, she moved back to L.A. She said that was where all her friends lived. The pull was just too strong. I never heard from Lashanda again.

Incarceration Crossroad

Drug addiction for my students did not discriminate between economic, cultural, ethnic, or family backgrounds. Of course, some of my students who lived with their biological parents also battled this debilitating problem. However, substance abuse rates are up to 50% higher for youths diagnosed with Conduct Disorder or Post Traumatic Stress Disorder (PTSD), who are living in larger residential facilities, or those leaving the child welfare system to live independently in transitional housing (Vaughn et al 2009). In turn, mental illness and alcohol or drug use are also frequent crossroads to incarceration for juveniles.

According to results of an extensive study conducted by Data Children's Network (DCN), of every person incarcerated under the age of 25 in California for the years 2014 and 2015, 43% reported a history of abuse, 18% had a history of intense levels of abuse, and 9% had been placed in the foster care system at some point in their lives (Cdnadmin 2017). The Sentencing Project in Washington D.C. found that in 2015 there were 6,726 juveniles in custody in California (State-by-State 2019). If we apply the same data trend as that of DCN's study, then approximately 2,892 juveniles in detention facilities had at least some type of reported maltreatment in their past, 1,211 had experienced intense abuse, and 605 had lived in foster care some time in their childhood. Incarceration is also more likely to be experienced by youths who live in areas with, "...higher rates of poverty and inadequate housing, health care, and other resources..." (Juvenile Felony 2019). Furthermore, "Youth of color...and... LGBTQ youths...are also consistently over-represented at every stage in the justice system" (Kids Data 2019).

One of the main pathways for children living in urban centers to getting involved in crime is through gang affiliation. Reasons for joining a gang can include the desire for status, protection, and/or a feeling of belonging to a family-like network (Why Young 2020). Since one of the chief activities of gangs is the sale and distribution of narcotics, many of these youths end up getting arrested at some point (Why 2020). Tragically, joining a gang can lead to a lifetime of running from the law and many gang members do not even live past the age of 20 (Zivanovic 2014).

In 2017, California's Department of Juvenile Justice (DJJ), published a report that showed 74.2% of youths arrested are re-arrested (Washburn 2017). Of these incarcerated juveniles, approximately 70% had a diagnosable mental illness. Examples were substance abuse/addictive disorders, Bi-polar disorder, Depression, Anxiety, Attention Deficit Disorder, and Post-Traumatic Stress Disorder (OJJDP 2017).

What is the response of our American legal system to the fact that many of our neediest children end up in trouble with law enforcement? There are many juvenile justice programs across the United States which focus on rehabilitation for non-violent offenders, rather than on jail time. However, despite the assumption of many adults that this is the most humane response to juvenile offenders, according to the U.S. Department of Justice-Office of Juvenile Justice and Delinquency and Prevention (OJJDP), many of these programs are poorly managed and not working in terms of deterring continued delinquency.

Surprisingly, recidivism, or the rate of return to probation, due to continued alcohol and/or drug abuse, is actually higher for youths assigned by judges to therapy-based juvenile court substance abuse programs (therapeutic treatment) than for those given straight punished-based probation (U.S.DOJ-OJJDP 2015). These statistics might lead to the conclusion that delinquent teens, who often have very low impulse control, require discipline and boundaries to reverse their life courses from negative to positive. In other words, they need a deterrent.

Interestingly, only 30% of Americans who even start in therapeutic type drug rehab programs actually finish them and the private nature (i.e. the physician-patient privilege), of therapeutic interventions makes them very difficult to investigate in terms of their effectiveness (Drug Rehab 2020). I witnessed the almost miraculous outcomes of some of my students whose parents paid big bucks to send them out of California to lock-up programs in other states which provided alcohol and drug rehabilitation therapy coupled with a strict regimen. Every one of those students returned to tell me that it was the best thing that their parents could have ever done for them. I wonder why we do not provide our delinquent teenagers in California with what really works in terms of real-life changes.

Permissive policies do not work as long-term deterrents to misbehavior for adolescents. In fact, permissive parenting (and in the case of foster and probation youth, who have the juvenile courts, caretakers and educators step in as their "parents"), can actually result in higher levels of misconduct, aggression and substance abuse, as well as lower levels of academic achievement, self-control, positive decision-making and social skills. These children are not taught important limits in their early formative years (Cherry 2019). I saw this unfortunate and predictable scenario play out innumerable times with my students over the last two decades.

Take for example, the David and Margaret Youth and Family Services program (D&M) in La Verne, CA, for teen girls from child protective services and probation, where I started my teaching career in 1993. It was shut down by the state in the fall of 2019, due to chaotic behavior on campus and in its transitional housing residences for young adults moving into independent living. D&M originally opened on June 28, 1910, as an orphanage for boys and girls of all ages. For 109 years, the staff there provided shelter, food, therapy, and education to children from all over Los Angeles County. However, as emotional disturbance and behavior issues of the clientele placed at D&M by county social workers elevated, so did lawlessness. The misbehavior of some of the teen girls (and the boyfriends from out of town who could be easily contacted on the girls' state provided cell phones), included rampant running away, violence both on campus and in the nearby quiet upper middle class community, sex trafficking, sale and use of narcotics, and finally a murder (Agrawal 2019).

I was even told by a former coworker of mine that the conduct of the D&M residents was so outrageous and frequent that the local La Verne Police Department stopped responding to the staff's phone calls for help. It could be easy to blame the staff for the lack of control, but what could they realistically do? The front and back gates to the facility were always open until late at night, residents could and would climb over the walls when the gates were locked, physically restraining clients was not permissible, and very few consequences were ever distributed by county social workers or probation officers in recent years for the youths' poor actions.

However, it was not always that way. I can remember that in 1993, when I first started working at Joan Macy School on the grounds of D&M, if a resident ran away, then her bed was

178

immediately closed and she was not allowed to return. That consequence was a deterrent to running away. Now, due to the shortage of quality residential programs for teens and the emergency level shortage of transitional housing available for young adults in California, runaways and students acting out are often allowed to either remain at or return to their group home facilities.

Conversely, at the end of January, 2020, as a member of a Western Association of Schools and College (WASC) Committee sent to the Kern County's Alternative Education program in Central California, I was privileged to witness a program in California which does seem to be successful in terms of providing not only order for juvenile offenders (many who have been foster children at some point in their lives), but hope as well. They attain a fresh vision for a different future in the form of job training and college classes in high school. Honestly, I was expecting out-of-date facilities and students working on droll packets of printed worksheets but was utterly pleased to see Kern Co. prove me wrong.

Now, there were certainly areas for improvement which our team identified with the district's leadership, but the school program passed accreditation with flying colors. There were three things which impressed me the most:

1. Clean, attractive, modern, calm, and orderly learning environments.
2. Positive interactions between school staff and students.
3. Job and career training.

The first location we visited was the Blanton Education Center, Kern Co. Alternative Education's largest community school campus, located in Bakersfield, CA. It provides both education and counseling services for students in grades K to 12 who are referred to them from other schools within the Kern County Superintendent of Schools District. Reasons for referral can include excessive absences, possible expulsion, or being on probation after release from incarceration. Blanton has a good reputation in the area and some parents want to enroll their struggling students there just due to its small class sizes and proven positive outcomes (Schools, KC 2020).

There was also one community high school on the Blanton campus that appeared more like a traditional continuation high school setting with an open campus setting, multiple classrooms, and small class sizes. The focus of its school staff was on enabling students to earn credits towards graduation which included a career/college pathways class and a Child Development Class in which any teen mothers attending the school could receive free childcare. Staff supervision was visible, but there were no police officers (only a metal detector at the front door).

The second school on the Blanton campus was a court school limited to students on probation. I saw about seven probation officers who greeted our committee at the locked front gate and only two classrooms of high school students with a total of 25-30 students in each. It struck me that everyone I met or spoke to was smiling. Now, I know they were all probably asked by their administrators to put their best foot forward for our visit, but there was an obvious vibe of peace and order on the unique campus in addition to a focus on learning. Student leaders proudly spoke about their school and showed off their hands-on projects, such as blankets they made for a community service project and sturdy, lacquered, wood toolboxes they made in the Construction Class.

Finally, the third school setting that I viewed in Kern County was an hour drive outside of Bakersfield, on a narrow and winding road up into the mountains in a starkly beautiful, simple little town called Kernville. The program was very different from the other schools that I had seen or had ever experienced in my career for that matter. It was called Camp Erwin-Owen, "...a 65 bed juvenile forestry (work) camp for (male) youth aged 14-18", who are on probation and which promotes, "...discipline, a strong work ethic and individual responsibility" (Camp Erwin 2013).

As would be expected, there was an obvious presence of probation officers all over campus and students were escorted everywhere they went on the grounds. The juvenile detainees wore brightly colored orange and blue prison style uniforms (I was informed that each youth received just one set of clothes upon their arrival). They also had their heads shaved, walked in military style formation, and answered, "Yes, Sir/Ma'am," or "No, Sir/Ma'am."

At the camp, students received an education, training in automotive repair and metal work (with a highly trained/experienced teacher and in a large, impressive auto shop), the opportunity to earn early college units, individual or family counseling (if the staff could convince a parent to drive that far), and substance abuse intervention. Besides school, the teens' jobs at Camp Erwin-Owen included maintaining the grounds, working with the chickens and pigs, gardening which provided for their dining hall, assignments in laundry or the kitchen, or service projects in the surrounding community.

At first, I had mixed feelings about the high level of control I saw at the detention camp. I knew from working with difficult teenagers that some of them would obviously rebel against such extreme levels of control placed upon them. We were informed that day, matter of fact, by a probation officer, that detainees did sometimes try to run away, but they always returned after a while due to the remote location, the cold temperatures at night and the eerie sounds of wildlife. Yes, initially, I felt uncomfortable with seeing children being treated like adult criminals.

Yet, by the end of our WASC tour of the detention program, I could see benefits of imposed discipline. I concluded that the youths placed at the camp were still criminals. Some had committed very serious and violent crimes, and the forced discipline was not only what they needed at the time to learn and receive consequences for their crimes but was also resulting in at least some positive outcomes for them. For instance, their Auto Shop teacher told us stories that morning about previous students of his that had moved on to take an Automotive Repair Class at a community college. Furthermore, according to the work camp's director, in 2018, the boys who leave and return to their home communities, "...recommit crimes only 33 percent of the time, whereas recidivism rates at the state DJJ (Department of Juvenile Justice) institutions are at 70-80 percent" (Teofilo 2018).

Nonetheless, our WASC visiting committee members were informed by the director of the remote detention facility that Camp Erwin-Owen was in danger of being closed by the State of California due to a declining census because the youths were being placed in therapeutic-based programs instead by their probation officers. In my opinion, that was a true shame and another illustration of the current trend in our nation to promote policies which focus on treatment without locking juvenile offenders up. This policy might appear to be compassionate at first glance, but it is neglectful if it puts the children themselves at additional risk of harm or results in a continued cycle of criminal activity which risks the safety of the rest of us in the larger society.

Nonetheless, probation departments across California are being mandated to move in this direction. In fact, Los Angeles County alone closed nine juvenile halls in the years 2017 to 2019, to focus on community-based interventions. However, there is a fundamental need to cut costs. In support of these changes, Sheila E. Mitchell, Probation Chief Deputy for Juvenile Services, said, "These cost-effective moves have consolidated staffing resources, moved youth closer to population centers in the County, allowed us to invest further in diverting youth away from the justice system, and expanded the trauma-informed, child-centered approach that is the L.A. Model to all of the remaining juvenile facilities" (Webb 2019).

I was curious to find out how much it costs taxpayers to house one juvenile delinquent in a juvenile hall or detention camp and some other reasons larger youth institutions are getting a beastly reputation in the public. I discovered in an article written by Jill Tucker and Joaquin Palomino, "Juvenile Hall Costs Skyrocket", in the *San Francisco Chronicle*, April 26, 2019 issue, that even though the census in juvenile halls has recently been cut in half, the inflation rate in the last eight years for incarcerating one youth in California has doubled. It costed taxpayers an unbelievable average of $284,700/year to keep one youth in juvenile hall in 2018. The highest amount that same year for juvenile detention, though, was paid in Santa Clara, an area South of San Francisco; the cost was $531,400/year per offender!

Besides skyrocketing costs, there are other factors state officials have considered in the decision to systematically close juvenile halls and detention camps across California. These facilities were originally intended for delinquents, ages 8 to 18, and the average length of stay has been 20 weeks (GPM 2020).

That is a long time for a child to be locked up in a place with a high incidence of violence, and often exacerbates feelings of PTSD, which they already had when they arrived (Newell and Leap 2013).

Those working inside of the detention centers have also provided insight into a daily terrifying tumult: busted walls and ceilings decorated with graffiti, broken cell phones littering the floor, fighting between rival gang members, and accusations against staff of child abuse for use of pepper spray. The detention officers are often reluctant to restrain the youths due to accusations of abuse from them and the general lack of consequences given to the prisoners. According to Deputy Chief Probation Officer Sheila Mitchell, "...officers no longer have the option of penalizing youths (in juvenile detention facilities), for acting out, such as limiting their time in common areas or reducing their allotted time for outside calls" (Stiles 2019). Moreover, the staff rarely tells anyone about the chaos due to fear of retaliation from those in leadership positions. Staff in juvenile halls have reported that they have plenty of staff members but are fed-up and afraid; these employees are so maxed out that they frequently do not show up for work.

Robert

Robert was a handsome, Black, powerfully built, 6' 4", 165 pounds, 18-year-old, and my student at Chaparral High for only three months. He had been placed at Hayne's Family Program in January of 2019 by his probation officer after serving his time in a juvenile hall. We had an immediate connection even though we had little in common in terms of backgrounds. Robert was a member of a street gang in Los Angeles whereas I was a middle-aged, middle class, White female teacher from the suburbs.

What impressed me most about Robert was how he restrained his strength and demonstrated gentleness and respect towards me and the other staff members. He also had a rare, sweet smile and worked harder than any of my other students. For instance, he decided to complete a senior project about his life and goals of pursuing a career in Construction, as well as present it in front of judges, although it was not a requirement for him. The following was Robert's personal statement about his life from his presentation:

Hello, my name is Robert Smith. I used to run the streets all day when I was younger doing bad things, but now my friends say I am very reliable, and they can count on me. My Mom says I am reliable and intelligent. My family says I'm a warrior. I say I am all those things and have a strong caring heart. My greatest talents are playing football and basketball and adjusting to what life throws at me. I've had a lot of changes and I've been through a lot.

Many memories define who I am as a person today. I was in and out of the system as a kid because the decisions I made were bad. This made me strong but sometimes I was lonely missing my family. My Mom loved me very much, but I also wondered about my Dad. He and my mom were separated when I was 11. I fondly remember playing football as a kid and my first job as a janitor.

Recently, my experiences as a new dad gave me concern for others. The most important thing in my life is my son. My goal is to be there for my son and be a great dad. My mom is second most important to me. Having a mom who has always been there for me right or wrong made me very thankful. I am also thankful for my seven older sisters. Next, my homies and homegirls are a huge part of my life. I also enjoy shooting dice, boxing, and freestyle rapping to myself sometimes. These are the things I spend my time and energy on.

In the next 5-10 years, I see myself changing in a better way. I might be married. I might even have more kids. I would enjoy having more kids. My girlfriend and I have been together for 3 years and I see us continuing to be best friends. However, I still have goals or dreams for myself. I am working on getting my high school diploma. I am trying to get experience, so I can be a professional boxer. But, for now, I enjoy being a student.

The people who have inspired me the most towards success are: Mom, Myself, Sisters, Cousins, & Teachers.

Robert earned an "A+" in my English Class until the day arrived when it was time to say goodbye; he had completed his probation and was returning to his home, family, and homies in L.A. On his final day with us, Robert stood in my classroom, and silently looked down at me with his big, round, beautiful brown eyes. I asked the gentle giant if I could give him a hug; Robert wordlessly nodded, and I quickly embraced my student. I then took Robert's boxing, big-knuckled right hand in between my two thin ones, and pleaded with him, "Robert, please make good decisions for yourself when you go home. I want to get pictures of your baby boy and updates on how well you are doing. You should probably move out here with your girlfriend and son, away from L.A., but I know you want to go home." That is the last memory I have of my vibrant, strong student, Robert; he was so full of promise.

I was just ending a dreamlike trip to Ireland with my husband in July, 2019, when I received a phone call at 4 p.m. from California; it was my co-teacher at Chaparral High School informing me that Robert was dead and telling me where I could find a news article about his death. I found a brief news article online just four sentences in length about an 18-year-old man named Robert who was shot and killed at 4 a.m. on the streets of L.A. while allegedly attempting to rob someone sitting inside a car.

I thanked my co-teacher for calling me, sat down on the white feather down comforter in my room at the bed and breakfast hotel in which my husband and I were staying, and wept. I still grieve for Robert. His death would be a motivator for me to ask my husband recently to pursue fostering/adopting again. I could not save Robert, but maybe I can help prevent another young man from getting trapped in a lifestyle of futility.

STRTP Trend

Tragically, Robert would not be my only student who died in the prime of his life. However, the next student I lost died while under the supposed full-time care of paid staff at Haynes Family Program, a local Short-Term Residential Therapeutic Program (STRTP). Many of the recent students from L.A. who are enrolled at Chaparral Continuation High School in San Dimas, CA, have resided in the two STRTPs for boys in our area: Haynes' Family Program and McKinley's Children's Center.

Most of these teens have a history of multiple foster homes, learning disabilities, and mental health issues. Some were arrested due to violent or harmful behaviors, such as robbery with a weapon, kidnapping, narcotics use or distribution, arson, rape, carjacking, gun possession, attempted murder, or murder (Juvenile Delinquency 2020). Now, because of recent shifts in policy that I mentioned earlier, instead of being locked up, these youths are being placed in STRTPs located within unsuspecting family neighborhoods.

I did a little research on STRTPs. According to the January 2, 2018 update of the *County of Los Angeles, Department of Children and Family Services and Probation Department Short-Term Residential Therapeutic Programs Foster Care Placement Services Contract),* the County of L.A., "... seeks to collaborate with its community partners to enhance the capacity of the health and human services system to improve the lives of children (ages 0-17), and families." It goes on to explain that a STRTP, "...means a residential facility that provides an integrated program of specialized and intensive care and supervision, services and supports, treatment, and short-term 24-hour care and supervision to children." The contract further explains that L.A. County's priorities for children living in placement are the following: (1) Safety, (2) Permanency, and (3) Access to effective and caring services (County of L.A. 2018). Basically, according to AB 403, a law passed in 2015 by the California Legislature, STRTPs are intended to be, "...integrated programs of high quality, therapeutic interventions and 24-hour supervision on a short-term basis for children who have complex and severe needs" (CDSS 2018).

Requirements to qualify as a STRTP are outlined by the California Department of Social Services in the *Short Term Residential Therapeutic Program Interim Licensing Standards, Chapter 7.5, Version 3.* The in-depth, 257-page handbook includes, among many other items, descriptions of an application for a license, criminal record clearance, issuance of a license, inspections, evaluations, accountability, personnel requirements, intake procedures, personnel duties, removal/transfer procedures, personal rights, discipline procedures, and trauma-informed intervention and treatment practices (CDSS 2019). These licensing requirements are obviously extensive and getting approval takes a great deal of time.

A fact ignored by most in this process is that caregivers in STRTPs are being asked to work with children with profound needs, but still getting paid minimum wage. They also do not always receive adequate training (as revealed by the public, posted employees' comments for any STRTP facility in any given area on glassdoor.com or indeed.com). This combination is not only highly unethical and irresponsible; it can be deadly.

Again, the purpose of STRTPs is that foster and probation youth of all ages who have intensive behavioral and/or mental health needs receive treatment in a more therapeutic setting and only for a temporary time. They are to be placed in a family setting as soon as possible, such as an extended family member's home or a foster family home. Moreover, STRTPs are not intended for foster or probation children who do not have extreme behavioral or mental health needs. Unfortunately, however, as there is a dire shortage of foster homes in California, especially ones who are willing to accept teenagers, social workers and probation officers often have no choice but to place lower needs children in the same setting as those with greater disturbance. These youths are then unintentionally exposed to a myriad of dangerous behaviors. A great emphasis is also placed on the idea of STRTP placements as being short-term; the maximum length of stay is supposed to be six months. However, if there is nowhere else to place a child, then a social worker or probation officer can file for an extension (Loxton 2019).

Another current egregious oversight on the part of California policy makers in terms of promising quality care for children in STRTPs is not having a plan for the education of these foster and probation youths. Public school districts in California, such as Bonita Unified School District (BUSD), in San Dimas, are legally responsible for providing a free and appropriate education to all the foster and probation youths in STRTPs located within their geographical boundaries. Not only that, but the recent laws protecting these children's rights require that they be enrolled in a school district immediately after placement. The result is that public school districts in California have been completely blindsided by the high level of needs of these new students simply dropped off at their schools' doorsteps. Not only that, but these school districts have been provided no assistance whatsoever by the state in terms of additional training for school staff or additional funding to hire more specialized teachers, counselors, campus supervisors, social workers, or probation officers. California is saving shiploads of money as they close juvenile halls and move to the STRTP model of care; it would only be both reasonable and responsible to share some of these savings with public school districts who now find themselves without any warning needing to provide an education to students of all ages with extreme behavioral, emotional and mental health needs.

Moreover, local community members should be aware that STRTPs, both 6-bed homes and larger residential facilities, are not locked; the high needs youths can walk off campus and into their surrounding communities whenever they feel like it. Not only has this added financial, morale, and safety concerns for school administrators and local law enforcement officers in terms of ensuring the welfare of existing students, their staff, themselves and the rest of their communities, but the children from STRTPs are also feeling the strain. The already traumatized children experience compounded stress and anxiety by being forced to attend yet another public school in an area with staff and students with whom they are not only unfamiliar, but with whom they initially feel like they have nothing in common. It can make for a volatile situation indeed.

I saw this phenomenon firsthand as a teacher, starting in February 2019, at Chaparral Continuation High School. Our district, BUSD, started receiving students from our local STRTPs with much more intensive needs and more frequently than ever before. It was nothing new for us to be working with foster and probation students from all over L.A. County, many from the City of L.A., gang members, and students with special needs. However, the emotional volatility and extensive lack of impulse control of some of these recent students were at unprecedented highs.

Not only that, but the STRTP students were arriving at Chap almost daily and being dropped off by residential staff with very little communication. I do want to mention that all of these students have the right in California to attend a school of choice, such as the last one they attended, in order to lessen the negative impacts of multiple moving of schools; however, it is clearly more convenient for both the youths and the staff who have to transport them, to attend a public school near where they currently live. Additionally, many of these facilities have schools on their campuses, but only students who have already qualified for Special Education and have a diagnosis of Emotional Disturbance can legally attend them. It is highly probable that many of the students being transferred from juvenile hall could actually qualify for special education services under a learning disability or emotional disturbance, but most likely, these youths either do not have anyone advocating for them in any meaningful way to refer them for educational testing or they do not stay in one school long enough to finish the assessment process if it was ever started.

Approximately 30% of our students at Chaparral High School were from local group homes which were later redesignated as STRTPs; most of them previously released from a juvenile hall or other placement and who originally resided in various sections of the inner city of Los Angeles. The ethnicities of STRTP students we served were generally White, Black/African American and Latino with the Whites being the smallest group in numbers. Until David & Margaret Youth and Family Services' STRTP was shut down in 2019, the breakdown of genders was about ⅔ male and ⅓ female. The rest of our students were from families in the suburbs of San Dimas and La Verne, CA, who were mostly White or Hispanic with a few being Black. A majority of our students had fallen behind in credits for graduation for a wide variety of reasons, such as truancy, lack of effort, finding themselves overwhelmed on a comprehensive high school campus, or impactful circumstances in their families over which they had little control. Others attended Chaparral High due to behavioral or social issues at a previous school. On the other hand, some attended simply because they preferred the smaller, more individualized educational program the staff could offer. There was also the added incentive that students were required to complete classwork only; no homework was assigned.

Thus, the variety of students we served at Chaparral was nothing new for us. Conversely, the increased high intensity of behavioral, emotional and mental health issues was definitely something we had to figure out quickly as the STRTP students started arriving in February 2019. Generally, most of our students, including those from foster or probation facilities, were respectful, kind, and talented. They definitely had some challenges and many had made poor decisions in the past, but once they settled into our positive and unique educational setting, they thrived academically, emotionally and socially (at least during the structured hours of the school day). Actually, as a teacher, I found that 17 or 18-year-old teenagers, especially the males, were really just little children inside big bodies who still craved for a word of praise, a tangible incentive reward, someone to laugh at their jokes, genuine friendship, free snacks, a listening ear, or maybe even a hug. These youths had been so brutally hurt and disappointed by peers and adults in their past and present lives, they just masked their emotional needs with hyperactivity, sullenness, anger, or withdrawal.

Nonetheless, quite a few of the students who enrolled immediately at our school after being placed in a local STRTP facility, had disruptive behaviors which were way beyond what our teachers, teachers' assistants, nurse clerk, campus supervisors, counselors, office personnel and administrators had dealt with previously. For instance, I will never forget Lucy, a female student I had who was on juvenile probation and living at D&M. She was the loudest and most brazen student I think I have ever known in my 20 years of education. If she had not been so exhausting and disruptive to everyone's school day, I might have found her almost comical. Lucy thought she had a God-given right to have lengthy cell phone conversations out loud while smacking her gum and waving her arms wildly around in the middle of my class and whenever she felt like it. She really had no shame at all. Lucy was actually a beautiful young lady, but also spoke with a strong accent, using a lot of slang, and dressed and applied her makeup heavily like she was from the streets of Los Angeles. Most of the time, although annoying, Lucy was harmless, until the day when she and two of her friends from the girls' placement decided to jump one of the girl's boyfriends in front of school while waiting for their van to pick them up. He did survive and the girls were suspended from school.

In February of 2019, some of the male students from the STRTPs arrived at our school with serious academic gaps and/or learning disabilities, PTSD from being systematically and recently abused and/or exposed to violence, explosive anger, poor impulse control, a desire to prove themselves on campus by fighting, and addiction to illegal substances. STRTPs receive from the State of California approximately $12-13,000/month for each child under their care. Out of this payment they promise to provide these children with intensive therapy; however, this does not always happen quickly or students refuse to participate in the process.

Not only were students from residential facilities immediately enrolled in our district, many coming to our continuation school, but they usually did not stay longer than 3-6 months. Just when we could see students from STRTPs making solid progress, be it assessment for Special Education services, school-based therapy, developing positive rapport, academic and social achievements, and/or earning credits towards high school graduation (quite frequently for the first time in one or two years), they would leave. The youths' required time for probation was fulfilled and they got to go home, or a few lucky ones had social workers who were finally able to find a more family-like foster home for them. There were also plenty of students who ran away from their placements.

Unfortunately, a portion of the teens from STRTPs, both female and male residents, found a new and easy source of sales for their narcotics: nice, suburban kids who had money in their pockets from mommy and daddy. One day, in fact, we had an 11th grade, female student on my Special Education caseload from a STRTP who frequently refused to attend school, walk by herself three miles so that she could get to school. The STRTP staff alerted our school administrators to the girl's suspicious behavior and she was found to be in possession of a large grocery bag full of marijuana. I can clearly remember the Manifestation Determination IEP meeting I held for her soon after that incident in which her mother, who had traveled all the way from L.A. with a younger sibling, remarked, "Here DCFS takes my daughter away from me because they say I cannot keep her safe and then this happens. Who was keeping her safe at her group home? Who supplied her with those drugs?" Of course, we could not answer her questions and proceeded with the meeting. That student eventually went through an expulsion process. However, while driving around our town, I saw her freely roaming the local community doing as she pleased while ditching school.

Drugs on campus was not our only serious concern; there was always the possibility that simmering tempers might flare into physical violence. Sometimes this anger was directed at teachers or teachers' assistants who placed expectations on these students to complete assignments and participate in class to earn credits. At other times, this anger was directed at their peers, both those from placement and local teens (some with their own nearby gang affiliations). Surprisingly, our local teens were most often the instigators of fights. Students secretly used their cell phones to communicate through text message to their homies when a rival peer was going to be out of class, so that they could plan an attack out in the open for everyone to see. Our staff tried to quell the use of cell phones, but it was a frequent frustration. We also responded quickly to any disputes, but they could end in some type of injury and a school suspension or expulsion, depending on the circumstances.

Clearly, the behavior of some of the STRTP students, or the combination created when they mixed with our local population, created some safety concerns and increased stress levels for both students and staff. Besides the threat of violence, many of these new students exhibited emotional and/or mental disturbances. Some of us, such as the foster and probation youth liaison, were spending a large part of our day counseling students who refused to stay in class, wanted to hurt themselves, or showed signs of deep depression. Our school and district administrators scrambled to meet in the Spring of 2019 to discuss ideas for immediate systems to put into place to alleviate these issues presenting themselves to our school staff almost daily.

However, "quickly" and "educational systems" are definite oxymorons; any kind of high-level decision-making involves multiple meetings and school board approval. I do have to say our principal, Christine Black, and the Bonita Unified School District administrators who were responding to her requests, including our superintendent, Carl Coles, did work as speedily as they could. Meanwhile, our Chaparral High School staff supported one another and did the best we could for the rest of the challenging 2018-19 school year.

Fortunately, Mrs. Black was able to get grant funding for the following 2019-20 school year which provided the ability to set-up a new classroom at Chaparral High with a teacher and teacher's assistant; it was called the, "Bridge Class". There was no assistance offered to our school at all through the state or federal government to assist with providing the educational needs of our intense STRTP students; our district was on its own. The principal was able to hire a credentialed teacher who had valuable experience with teen students in crisis. The Bridge Class was intended to be short-term and included the following four main purposes:

1. Increase the overall safety of all students and staff, including lowering recently rising stress levels.
2. Give students suddenly being dropped off at our school from traumatizing situations at their new STRTPs time to adjust to their new school environment as well as learn the academic and behavior expectations they needed to follow in order to be successful.
3. Gather crucial information about the students so that we could better provide them access to their education, such as reading and math assessments,

transcripts/credits earned from previous schools, IEP documents (for those receiving Special Education services), emotional triggers, and strengths/weaknesses, etc.

4. Prepare these students to enter our regular program of classes at Chaparral as soon as they demonstrated through their behavior and attitude that they were ready (sometimes this happened with just one or two classes, but others were ready for a full-day fairly quickly).

We generally received one of two extremes of students at Chap from the STRTPs, in terms of credits earned. About half of these teen students had missed a tremendous amount of school and were one to two years behind in credits towards their high school graduation; the other half had only a handful of credits left to complete when they arrived on our school's doorstep. Even though they had experienced on-going trauma, including multiple moves throughout their childhoods, many of the students had somehow been able to focus on schoolwork. Actually, for countless teens from the foster or probation systems, since our school was managed with integrity, love, and clear guidelines, it was the one place they could count on for stability, safety, peace, and acceptance for seven hours out of every weekday. Of course, we had no control over what happened to our students once they walked out of our gates or on the weekends.

Jack

On a May afternoon in 2020, during COVID-19 quarantine and school closure, I answered another phone call from my teaching partner at Chaparral High School. She tearfully told me that 18-year-old Jack, a recent graduate from our school and resident of the local large STRTP group home, Haynes Family of Programs, died at 5 a.m. that morning. His staff had found him lying on his bedroom floor and he could not be revived. The cause of death was thought to be a heart attack, but narcotics were found both in his clothing and hidden in his room. I cried once again for the tragic death of one so young; he was a student who had survived endless heartache and had received from our school staff vast amounts of love.

When I knew Jack, he had curly light brown hair and a bushy beard. However, what stood out the most about him to me was his radiant smile. For a teenager who had suffered so much growing up, his cheerfulness was truly a testimony to his spirit of endurance. Jack was also kind and respectful to both his peers and school staff. He lived among violent and deeply disturbed youths at his STRTP but did not display those behaviors himself at school. Jack was motivated to work hard and complete his graduation credits. On the downside, Jack was suspended from our school multiple times for bringing vaping devices or marijuana onto the school campus.

Jack was not enrolled in any of my classes, because he had earned enough credits and no longer needed an English class. Yet, I still had a fair amount of interaction with him because he was on my Special Education caseload; I managed his Individual Education Program (IEP), needs, meetings, and communications. Additionally, Jack's mother was the most difficult parent I had ever worked with during my teaching career. Jack had still been a minor, 17 years old, when he first arrived at our school, and his parents were creating an uphill battle for me in attempting to schedule his 30-day IEP meeting. I was required by law to have one of them attend the IEP meeting to provide input and consent. His father would answer my requests politely by email with very short responses, but never showed up at school for a meeting. Jack's mother never even responded to my communications sent by mail, and rarely answered the ones I sent via email or voicemail. Yet, I was legally unable to hold the important meeting without one of Jack's parents attending either by telephone or in person.

Finally, months after my initial attempt to reach her, Jack's mother called the school office and left me a voicemail message; I was then able to call her back to confirm her attendance at our now overdue IEP review meeting. Although 25 minutes late, she did show up to that meeting, but then proceeded to say to the IEP team seated around the long oval table, "I refuse to allow this meeting to proceed."

I asked Jack's mother if there was a reason why she was refusing to hold the IEP meeting.

Jack's mother started rambling about how she was suing the Los Angeles Unified School District (LAUSD). I explained to her that we were the Bonita Unified School District, not LAUSD. However, she replied, "I don't care; I refuse to allow this meeting." She then walked out of the meeting room. The interactions our school staff had with Jack's mom over the next

12 months went similarly, although sometimes her tone of voice and words were even more agitated.

During the following school year, when Jack turned 18, he was his own legal educational rights holder, and I no longer needed his father's or mother's permissions to hold a meeting or consent to his IEP document which included his special education goals and services. Frankly, I was relieved not to have his parents involved and expected Jack would be too. However, when I asked Jack if he still wanted to invite his mother and father to his annual IEP meeting, even though he did not have to, he said, "Yes." Once again, I saw in one of my students that even as a young adult, he desperately desired his parents' love and attention, even if it was imperfect. So, I invited his parents to his next meeting, but never heard from them. Jack willingly signed his own IEP papers that day.

Not only did Jack endure a childhood with a mother who appeared to possibly struggle with a mental illness, but he also attended more than 35 different schools. I cannot imagine how stressful that must have been for him. Moreover, although I wish Jack had chosen healthier coping mechanisms available to him, I was not surprised that he was trying to make himself feel better through the abuse of illegal substances. The reality, however, is that his use of alcohol or drugs to numb his pain, rather than learning healthy therapeutic coping strategies, made his feelings worsen and ultimately led to his death, just like too many other young Americans (Miller 2020).

Furthermore, Jack died while residing in a large STRTP residential facility, funded by taxpayers at approximately $12-13,000/month, which had promised California State in exchange for their operating license to provide quality, therapeutic, 24/7 supervision to all of its residents (CDSS 2016). The intentions of California policymakers in closing juvenile halls and requiring many former group homes to restructure in order to qualify as STRTPs, was to save money and supposedly focus more on therapeutic interventions for both foster and probation youth. Nonetheless, these children sometimes still tragically die when placed in out-of-home care. In fact, the Senate Finance Committee, in an unusual bipartisan maneuver, conducted a study of a different large, for profit, national foster care service in 2015, and found that 86 American children had died in the company's care over a 10-year span. Shockingly, the panel also found that the, "...death rate among foster children was found to be 42 percent higher than the national average". The investigating committee's high-ranking Democrat, Senator Ron Wyden, concluded that, "This is about denying the most vulnerable kids in America the chance to have healthy and productive lives" (Grim & Chavez 2017).

A tree was planted in Jack's name at his STRTP, Hayne's, after he died, and everyone went back to living their day to day lives. One of my co-workers told me to smile because Jack would not want us to be sad. I felt furious helplessness; I did not want to smile or forget the senseless loss of a child so promising. Some other teachers and I, however, decided to keep track of any complaints made against the residential facility by joining a public notification system which sends periodic emails. Last September 2020, I read that an investigation of Jack's death at the STRTP resulted in the police finding that my student choked to death on his own vomit after a drug overdose. It went on to say that if his two staff members on duty had been attentive, then they could have assisted him and possibly prevented his death. The two employees were fired, and further charges were being considered. The report further explained that the two people on duty that night originally lied to the police about their actions the events of the early morning of Jack's death. A video shows that the female staff member was sleeping while she was supposed to be checking on the children under her care and the male employee had left the campus altogether for several hours. Unfortunately, all the good done at a group home can be overshadowed by one such tragic incident.

Rights vs. Safety

When a child of any age is forcibly removed from his biological parents by a child welfare agency, what exactly are the responsibilities of the newly appointed and government funded caregivers? Basically, the idea is that foster parents, group home residential counselors, or adoptive parents will serve as nurturing substitute parents. The deplorable reality is that some of these children face further maltreatment at the hands of their paid guardians. The least possible danger posed to them is that they will be treated like second class citizens. They could also experience emotional, physical, or sexual abuse by the same adults paid and put into place to save them from such atrocities that occurred in their homes of origin.

Foster children can be so used to being abused, in fact, that they stop thinking anything is wrong with it and might not speak up for themselves by telling an adult in their lives about what is happening. Unfortunately, sometimes overloaded county social workers do not always visit each child on their caseloads every month as is expected of them or neglect to spend quality time alone with foster children which would provide them a clear picture of how the children are doing (Wexler 2018).

A female, 15-year-old student once told me that her foster mother would only allow her to walk in certain parts of the house: the bathroom, hallway, and her own bedroom. She also had to ask permission to get anything out of the refrigerator. She was not receiving a required monthly allowance from her foster mother either; after I told her to call her social worker, that suddenly changed. I was repeatedly perplexed about how my husband and I, as foster parents, seemed to be held accountable by social workers to follow countless county guidelines, but how so many others got away with substandard care.

One of the most unsettling circumstances I heard about was in an Individualized Education Plan (IEP) meeting that I was administering for a group home for an 11-year-old boy. The director did not give me all the specifics of why the boy was placed at the facility but did inform me that he had been removed from his adoptive parents. I then learned that he had revealed to staff that his adoptive parents had the custom of having him sleep in bed with them every night. I felt even more unsettled when I found out that the boy was still allowed by L.A. County DCFS to visit his adoptive parents on the weekends.

Unfortunately, it is also not uncommon for foster and probation youths to be exposed to on-going danger in larger group homes by the other children residing with them. This may include violence, thievery, drugs, and sexual abuse. Large caseloads and years of experience with the child welfare system can lead some social workers and probation officers to becoming jaded which can then result in inadequate monitoring of the children's safety (Babbel 2012).

In response to these types of failings in child welfare systems nationwide, federal laws were passed in the United States in the 1960s and 70s to spell out the rights of children taken from their families by a state's child protective services or juvenile justice system and placed in some type of foster care. It is a long list, but some of the rights of these children include the following:

- To live in a safe, healthy, and comfortable home where they are treated with respect.

- To receive adequate and healthy food, adequate clothing, grooming and hygiene products, and an age-appropriate allowance.
- To be free from unreasonable searches of personal belongings.
- To make, send, and receive confidential telephone calls and other electronic communications, and to send and receive unopened mail, unless prohibited by court order (California Law 2020).

Likewise, in 2003, California passed AB408, to clarify previous federal legislation to further protect the rights of children placed by the state into a foster or group home. Some of the newer legal lingo requires that these children be placed in the most "family-like" environment possible and be able to participate in social activities, etc., appropriate to their ages. Another safety measure added is that any of these youths' caregivers, including foster parents and group home staff, will "... use a **reasonable and prudent parent standard...**" (Foster Care 2019). According to the California Department of Social Services (CDSS), a **"reasonable and prudent parent standard"** is defined as, "...careful and sensible parental decisions that maintain the child's health, safety, and best interests..." (CDSS Programs 2020).

The ironic travesty I have witnessed time and again in my 20 years teaching students in the child welfare and juvenile justice systems is that laws written to protect the rights of children placed in out of home care can sometimes end up resulting in a colossal threat to children's well-being and safety if caregivers do not heed or are actually prevented from following the standard of using the **reasonable and prudent parent standard.** There is a modicum of common sense that needs to be followed when providing both privileges and necessary restrictions for youths in care, just like with any child. However, due to the threat of lawsuits and the lengthy process of acquiring court orders from a judge to take away any rights outlined by laws created to protect children, foster parents and group home staff will too often turn a blind eye to potentially dangerous situations; they feel as if "their hands are tied".

Take for example the right of all foster and probation youths in California to own a cell phone (free for them and paid for by tax dollars), to privately contact family members whenever they want. Although cell phones are amazing and convenient technological wonders of our modern age, I think most adults can see the potential downside of these communication devices for children in terms of distraction, obsession, loss of sleep, bullying, poor role models, etc.

However, for foster and probation youths, cell phones can be even more problematic. For instance, cell phones make it easy for pimps to reach young ladies in a group home to tell them to meet them at the front gate at 5 p.m. for a car ride, or allow juveniles struggling with addiction to quickly reach their dealers. Despite these dangers, laws in California say that a cell phone cannot be taken away from a juvenile in foster care or in custody; the only exception is if there is a court order authorizing caretakers to remove a phone (L.A. Co. DCFS 2019).

What about the logical idea of searching rooms to check for dangerous drugs or weapons? The children in foster homes or other placements have the right to be free of <u>unreasonable</u> searches of their personal property (FosterYouthHelp 2020). Any attempt on the part of a caregiver to challenge this right (or any right), must first be approved by a County Program Director (Foster Youth 2019). The mixed messages given to government funded caretakers can be very confusing and contradictory.

Take for example a group home staff member who knows a teen under his watch has a past history of illegal substance use; he is obligated to protect the safety of that child, but is also forbidden to search the child or his possessions without official authority. Any prudent parents with a child battling addiction would certainly conduct regular searches of their child's bedroom and that would not be considered unreasonable. Instead, those parents would be applauded for not only being reasonable, but lovingly trying to protect their child from himself. However, the laws in California which protect the rights of minors under the state's protection, sadly conflict with expectations for children's safety. Foster parents and residential staff are frequently caught up in this web of legal confusion. Basically, the written laws regarding juveniles and how they play out in real life yield messy and dangerous results.

I strongly believe that adults paid by the government to provide substitute parental care for children should be given the ability to protect these same children from themselves when necessary. Yes, this might just mean temporarily taking away a privilege, such as a cell phone. Does not every wise and caring parent provide restrictions for children when those children are acting irresponsibly? We would not blink if our neighbor told us that she took her teen daughter's cell phone away because the girl was contacting an adult man who had been having a sexual relationship with her. Neither would we argue the point if another neighbor took a cell phone away from her son, because he was struggling with an addiction to drugs. Why do judges and lawyers in California then slap the hands of foster parents or group home staff and tell them that they are being unreasonable when they attempt to apply similar prudent parenting standards to the foster and probation youths under their care? I think it ludicrous when California policymakers value personal liberties over protecting the lives of our most marginalized American children. I am fully aware that teens can just find ways around any restrictions placed upon them, but all responsible adults entrusted with safeguarding children can at least try to make it more difficult for them to engage in risky behavior. It could mean the difference between life and death, like in the case of my student, Jack.

Bella & Dolores

I suppose it was not too much of a jump to think that I might just go ahead and invite one of my foster students from my school home one day. In August 2018, my husband and I downsized from our large home in San Dimas, CA, to a smaller one in La Verne; except for our two dogs, we were empty nesters. Dave and I did not like our empty extra bedrooms and quiet house; thus, began step one in my plan for us to recertify as foster parents. I approached Dave with the words he had heard so often (poor guy), "Honey, I have an idea."

Dave thought about it for a few weeks, then agreed to start the recertification process. However, the second step in my plan (once again, poor Dave), was to transform the second unnecessary large living room in the back of our new home into a bedroom with two closets. After several months of workers, dust, noise, locking our dogs in our bedroom where our giant mutt chewed off the doorframe, and paying much more money to our remodeling crew than originally planned, our new beautiful and functional bedroom with double French doors was complete.

Step three involved calling Serenity Foster Family Homes, the agency we fostered through before, and telling them we were interested in fostering young adults who were getting ready to move into adulthood. They suggested we call the David and Margaret Foster Family Agency (FFA), because D&M had more experience with teen placements. Although the D&M residential program for foster and probation youths and the transitional program had been closed the previous fall, their foster agency was still operating. My husband and I liked the idea of still supporting D&M, where I had started my journey in teaching, and it was a convenient 3-minute drive from our home. Next, we attended an orientation and got yet another long list of things we needed to do to be approved to take a foster young adult into our home.

The experience was similar to the process we went through as prospective foster parents seven years earlier. We got our fingerprints and background checks completed (for the umpteenth time), locked up all our cleaning supplies, tools, and medicines, and installed additional smoke and monoxide detectors. However, we found that the L.A. County Department of Children and Family Services (DCFS), had added more requirements, not less. For instance, the ingredients list for our emergency preparation kit had grown; we had to buy a 19-gallon plastic container to hold everything, including a wind-up radio and an extra bag of dog food. They also asked us to hold in reserve 40 gallons of water; I decided to buy 12 gallons of bottled water instead and held my breath; no one ever said anything. Previously, the big deal while social workers inspected our refrigerator, was to make sure that we used NO tin foil on ANY food items. Conversely, this time around, there was no mention of tin foil, but we were asked to throw out any tin cans that had any dents in them.

All in all, Dave and I found the social workers at D&M's private FFA pleasant, supportive, and easy to work with throughout the entire process. Nonetheless, there was some confusion for all of us regarding expectations for foster parenting young adults, rather than underage minors. The FFA had not had too much experience with people showing up at their doorsteps asking to foster youths transitioning into adulthood; so, there were a few bumpy patches along the road, but we all learned together.

When Dave and I were getting close to finishing the FFA's approval process in the Spring of 2019, I when in search of Bella. She had been one of my 12th grade students the previous semester in an Economics Class in which I was a co-teacher. I quietly asked her if I could privately speak to her outside of the classroom for a minute, then told Bella that my husband and I were almost ready to be foster parents again. I asked her if she would just think about considering us for a new home and family to support her as she transitioned into adulthood and let me know her decision when she was ready. The 18-year-old smiled but did not say much. We went our separate ways.

There were many gaps in my knowledge about Bella's background. I did know that she was getting close to graduating, and was a quiet, shy, pretty, and sweet young, Black woman. In terms of the personal circumstances that had led Bella to be classified as a foster youth, I had been told that her mother had tragically passed away about nine months previously. Bella herself told me weeks later that she had also been in and out of foster care during her childhood, starting in the First Grade.

I did not hear back from Bella for several months after our initial conversation, although I passed by her and we smiled at each other daily in between classes. I was trying to avoid making her feel any awkward pressure and did not bring up the subject of her possibly being our foster daughter again. Eventually, I just assumed that Bella was not interested, but was too shy to tell me. However, one afternoon, Bella and one of her friends suddenly approached me at lunchtime, and with a big smile, Bella said, "I would like to come live with you." A little surprised, but pleased, I gave the teen my cell phone number and asked her to give it to her county social worker (CSW), so that she could call me. She also gave me her CSW's cell number which I passed onto our D&M FFA social worker who got the ball rolling. I also informed everyone that my husband and I would be able to have Bella join our family right after our planned 10-day trip to Ireland that July.

In the meantime, I prepared the bedroom for Bella; nesting for a 19-year-old is a little different than for a newborn baby, but I still had fun shopping for bedding, towels, and closet organizers. Bella and I also got together to get to know one another a bit more before becoming instant family members.

One evening, I took Bella out for Chinese food, but she ate very little. I wondered if she did not like the food, but she finally told me that her mouth hurt a lot and she was unable to eat much.

I asked Bella, "Why does your mouth hurt?"

Bella replied, "My teeth hurt a lot. It hurts to eat."

The mama bear's protective instinct in me went from level 1 to 25 within seconds and I asked, "Why haven't you gone to the dentist?"

Bella said, "Because I don't want to pay for it."

My protective instinct then jumped to level 50 and I said, "But, you have Medi-Cal, free health insurance, as a foster child; you don't have to pay for the dentist."

She looked at me with her round, beautiful dark brown eyes and said, "I don't have any health insurance; I haven't had any since my mom died nine months ago."

Now, my protective instinct reached 100 and questioned, "You have a social worker, right? Why don't you have a Medi-Cal card and health insurance?"

Bella said, "Yes; well, I don't know."

That moment was when I realized that I had entered Bella's life for a clear purpose; I was meant to help her with the basic necessities, no matter how long it might be.

The first thing she needed was to get to the dentist. Her best friend's mom kindly took Bella to a dentist for her first appointment, but I told Bella that she should call her CSW right away and tell him that she needed a Medi-Cal card immediately.

Bella got her insurance card at our house about one month later and I got busy making multiple dentist appointments for her. That initial request to her county social worker was probably also the beginning of a tension filled relationship I ended up having with him. I am sure, in fact, that I have a giant red star drawn next to my name at the local county DCFS office. However, the only thing that mattered to me was taking care of Bella.

After Dave and I got back from our trip to Ireland that summer, I called Bella and told her we were ready for her to move in. She sounded happy, then called me back a few minutes later to tell me that her CSW said she could move into our home the next day. I was surprised that it would happen so quickly but agreed. I really had no idea what the CSW was thinking, because he made no effort to communicate with me.

Bella and her social worker arrived at our home the next evening about 5 p.m. He stayed for about 15 minutes and informed me that he was her SILP worker, then proceeded to swiftly go down a checklist with Bella. He asked her if she felt capable of doing all of the independent living skills, including things like washing her own clothes, cooking for herself, finding her own transportation, getting a job, and going to school, etc. Bella, as was her usual way, just silently nodded in agreement.

After the CSW finally took a breath, I asked him a question that I thought was logical, "Isn't there any paperwork for us to sign?"

He replied, "No. You are Bella's landlords only. How much are you going to charge her for rent?"

I answered, "We are going to ask her to pay $400/month for all of her expenses, and she is always welcome to eat for free with us at home or when we go out."

He said, "That's very nice of you. Well, that's about it then."

I asked, "Do you want to see her bedroom?"

The CSW agreed, made some polite comments about the room, then left.

At that point, my confusion started setting in; the process we just went through was nothing like anything I had experienced with foster care in the past. However, I did not want to alarm Bella on her first night with us, so I did not say anything to her yet. A county SILP supervisor came the next day to approve our home for SILP placement. She stayed about 10 minutes and did not provide me with any paperwork either.

What I did not realize at the time was that SILP is not the same thing as foster care; it is an entirely different system and not what my husband and I had recertified for at D&M. Supervised Independent Living Placement (SILP), is a fairly new option available for non-minor dependents (NMDs) in L.A. County, ages 18-21, who were in foster care at least by the time they reached age 16 and who are ready to live completely independently; they are supposed to take care of ALL of their own needs. The youths can rent an approved apartment or bedroom in someone's home. However, the landlords are just landlords. Nothing else is expected of the receiving adults. Moreover, paperwork, communication from social workers, and support are not offered. The monthly $1,000 checks from the government go directly to the young adult foster youths; they have to use this money to learn how to budget, including paying for all of their bills in terms of rent, food, clothes, transportation, etc. (Children's Law Center 2013). If a youth in SILP qualifies and their CSW follows through for them, then he/she can also get a government funded food card to use at grocery stores. Of course, $1,000/month does not go very far, at least in Southern California, so SILP youths are encouraged to also find jobs to be able to start a savings account. The government stipends also stop at age 21.

I called our private FFA social worker soon after Bella moved in with us and explained what had happened with Bella's county social worker. I emphasized that my husband and I wanted the support of the private D&M foster family agency. We knew from experience, that CSWs, although often well-intentioned, were not always quick to respond to questions or requests. In other words, we had already firmly determined that we had to have the support of the FFA, not only for Bella's best interests, but for our own protection as well.

Continuing the phone call, I said that I was now realizing from Bella's behavior that she was going to initially require a great deal of time and assistance in getting things completed for her transition into adulthood. Although Bella had agreed to being capable of the long checklist with her CSW, her behavior was saying something else altogether. The FFA social worker encouraged Bella and I to first talk with Bella's CSW about changing her status from SILP to foster youth and promised that he would also reach out to the CSW.

I first spoke with Bella and explained the situation, that Dave and I really wanted her to continue to live in our home, but that we also needed to be a part of a foster agency. We went on to say that this would mean she would have to change her independent status from SILP to foster youth. That would also mean that we would be getting the $1,000 check each month, not her, but out of which we would give her a generous spending allowance, an additional clothing allowance, and provisions for all of her toiletries and food. I stressed that the decision was completely hers; if she decided to remain in SILP and to either find a new bedroom to rent or to move back to her uncle's home with her older sister, then I would still be available as a part of her support system. I asked Bella to think about it and said I would ask her again later that day.

Bella told me that afternoon that she wanted to be our foster child and remain with Dave and I in our home, so I called her CSW. He was immediately, adamantly opposed to the idea. In fact, he emphatically told me, "No, absolutely not. Bella is completely capable of living independently and I do not see how re-entering foster care will benefit her". He did not ask me any questions and that was the extent of our "conversation".

Next, I called our caring and capable FFA social worker back and told him about our ongoing dilemma. He told me that would speak with his supervisor at the D&M FFA and try to set-up a meeting at the nearest DCFS office with Bella, Dave and I, the county social worker, the county office supervisor, himself, and his D&M supervisor.

On the day of the meeting, as we drove five miles to the DCFS office in Pomona, I repeated to Bella that the decision about where she lived was completely in her control and that I would not be offended if she decided to be in SILP again. Although Dave and I would not be able to continue having her live with us, we would still offer to help her. I asked Bella again, "Are you sure you want to be a foster child again?"

Bella looked me in the eyes and quietly responded, "Yes, I do."

I told her, "Okay, then I will fight for what you want; this is all about you and what you want, no one else."

Next, Bella, Dave and I, walked into the cold, metal-framed, glass office building, down the familiar (from visits years earlier with our previous foster children), tile hallway, and into the busy DCFS office; we were asked by the unsmiling receptionist behind the desk and glass partition to sign-in and who we were there to see. I told her Bella's CSW's name and then we all sat down to wait. Her CSW and his supervisor came out of an inner office door after a few minutes. We were then asked to follow them down another inner hallway to a tiny room at the back of the office which was filled to the brim with a large round table and chairs. We all sat down and awkwardly attempted to make polite conversation while we waited for the D&M social worker and his supervisor to arrive which they did about 5 minutes later.

Bella's CSW tried to dominate the meeting; he started talking about how he thought foster care was a terrible idea for Bella and that she was completely capable of living on her own. He went on to say that he could not think of a single thing Dave and I could do to help Bella that she could not do for herself.

Inside my head, as all of us sat silently through his tirade, I wondered how the CSW could know so little about Bella if he had been her social worker for an entire year. Afterall, county social workers were required to meet with every youth on their caseload once each month; I found out later from Bella that had not been happening for her.

The CSW's body language at the meeting was both aggressive and defensive, and the worst part was that he never once paused to ask Bella what she wanted. I could not understand his obvious hang-up about foster care (or maybe he just did not like Dave and I; I really could not say), but after about 10 minutes of his abrasive speech, I found that I could not take it anymore. I was either going to have to get him to stop or leave the room completely. Furthermore, no one else was saying or doing anything, so I figured it was going to be up to me.

I interrupted Bella's CSW, made a little invisible left to right "dash" motion in the air with my right hand, and said, "I have really had enough; I cannot listen to you anymore."

The CSW leaned back in his chair, stared coldly at me, and asked, "Oh really, you've had enough?"

"Yes; besides, this decision is up to Bella. Why hasn't anyone asked Bella what SHE wants? Dave and I are here to support her in whatever she decides."

I then turned to my right and asked Bella, "So, Bella, what do you want? Do you want to stay in SILP or remain in our home as a foster child?"

Bella, easily intimidated at that juncture in her young life, quietly looked around at everyone around the table, then meekly answered in one word, "SILP."

I could only assume that Bella was afraid of upsetting her CSW and that her greatest desire at that moment was for the tense meeting to end.

Our FFA social worker then stepped in and asked Bella to explain why she wanted to stay in SILP; Bella did not respond.

I looked around the table at the group and said, "Well, that is fine; it is up to Bella. So, what is the next step for her then?"

The FFA supervisor replied, "I think we should give Bella one more week to make a final decision; this meeting might be uncomfortable for her." Everyone around the cramped room agreed.

Bella, Dave, and I then walked out of the office and into the parking lot with our FFA social worker and his supervisor. I told them that I had never been treated so rudely by a county social worker. They agreed that the meeting should have gone a lot differently.

The following week in our home, I did not bring up the meeting with Bella again because I did not want to put any pressure on her. It was my desire that Bella feel empowered to make her own decision. She ended up bravely calling her CSW one week after her meeting and telling him that she wanted to be our foster daughter. I did not hear their conversation, but she informed me later that her county worker argued with her, but that she had stood firm in her choice. I told Bella that I was proud of her, not for agreeing to what I thought was best for her (at least for the time being), but for standing up to someone intimidating. That was a huge step for Bella. Leaving the SILP program also meant that Bella was going to be assigned a different county social worker and that was a relief.

Overall, Bella was very easy to have in our home. She could take care of her daily routine and wash her own clothes, but I was still worried about her because she sat alone in her bedroom almost all day, every day, using social media or watching Disney movies on her cell phone. I was used to a nineteen-year old wanting to go out with friends, being noisy, and even messy. Bella, on the other hand, was quiet, extremely neat, and rarely communicated with us; she did not leave our home to go out anywhere for several weeks.

I tried to engage Bella in conversation by inviting her into the living room to play with our dogs or watch television with me, and I asked if she would like to eat dinner with Dave and I every night. I never saw Bella cook anything, except for boiling water for Top Ramen. Matter of fact, she ate and drank very little; this also concerned me.

Bella's reclusive behavior lasted nearly two months. It was very awkward for Dave and me at times; we kept trying to engage Bella, but she continued to mostly isolate herself. I am highly social, communicative, and energetic, so I started feeling anxious about her sedentary lifestyle; I knew we probably had opposite personalities, but I was troubled about Bella's physical and emotional health.

Bella was, however, willing for me to take her to numerous dental appointments as well as a physical and drug test required by the county. The physician reported that Bella was in general good health but needed to hydrate and eat more. That was already obvious.

One evening, as I was getting dinner ready, to my shock, Bella entered the kitchen, walked past me and then suddenly fainted; she hit her head on the granite counter and crumbled to the hardwood floor. I quickly bent down and rolled up a towel under Bella's head, then asked her how she was feeling. Her speech was slurred, and she appeared highly disoriented. I supported our foster daughter in walking to my car and then took her to an emergency room.

Bella ended up being okay, but she was given fluids through an IV, because she was extremely dehydrated. I told Bella on the way home in the car that I was going to be nagging her more about drinking and eating; although she was nineteen and I knew that she did not like me "bugging" her, I felt responsible for her well-being while she was a part of our family. I said she could get mad at me if she wanted to, but until I started seeing her take better care of herself, I was going to keep a closer eye on her.

Thankfully, things started to improve. Bella left her bedroom, played, and walked the dogs with us, ate dinner with Dave and I most nights, and accompanied me on errands, like grocery shopping. We also found a shared love of Zumba classes at the Gym. Bella still said very little, but I came to accept that it was just her way; I had to learn to discipline myself not to speak to cover up the gaps in conversation and be comfortable with silence when I was alone with her.

Bella also attended Foothill Church in Glendora on Sundays with us; it was totally her choice, but she went with us almost every week. Additionally, she decided to volunteer with Dave and I in the Toddler's Class at church two Sundays each month. Bella really enjoyed playing with the little ones and they loved her back. The three of us would always go out for lunch after church too.

Bella experienced quite a few "Firsts" as our foster daughter. She and I went together one Saturday, and she got her first pedicure. She also decided to start getting beautiful, long braids of varying colors every six weeks for the first time. I took her to get her first California Identification Card (studying for her driver's license would be next), and to the back to open her first checking account. I drove Bella to the Social Security Office to get another copy of her S.S. card, and showed her how to enroll in classes at Citrus Community College for the first time. Dave also bought Bella her first laptop computer for school and home.

Bella made a decision to major in Business and two afternoons, I drove her over to Citrus College before her first day of classes and we walked around, so that she could be confident about the location of her classes, the library, and the cafeteria, etc. We went shopping, Bella picked out a backpack and a few school supplies, and she appeared ready to go.

Regrettably, Bella's first day of college did not go well. I received a phone call from her that afternoon while I was at work, telling me that she hated her classes; she said the coursework was overwhelming and the other students were a lot older than her. She had dropped her classes and was heading home. I told Bella that I was so sorry about her negative experience, then dropped the subject.

A few days later, I brought up the subject of college again and suggested, based upon Bella's fondness for and great skills with the toddlers at church, that maybe she might want to think about a different major, such as Child Development. She could be either a preschool or elementary school teacher or a teacher's assistant, depending on how many classes she wanted to take.

Bella did decide to re-enroll at Citrus for the following semester with a major in Child Development. I drove her to the campus, and we walked around again, so that she could easily find her classes on the first day of the new semester. Thankfully, Bella had a completely opposite experience on her first day of classes this time around. She even excitedly called me after her classes were over that day to tell me how well everything had gone and that some of the other students were even familiar to her from high school days. Not only that, but some of them had asked her to go out to dinner with them after classes were over! I was so happy for Bella and told her I was proud of her.

Bella passed that first class at Citrus with flying colors, then went on the next semester to pass three more classes. I asked Bella how many classes she was going to take, and she answered, "I don't know; I'm just going to keep taking them." She also told me that her oldest sister had just graduated from a university and was proud of her too.

As a result of the success and confidence Bella was developing both in our home and at school, our foster daughter was also blossoming socially; she was hanging out more with her friends and siblings. To increase her independence, Bella usually took Uber transportation anywhere she needed to go. Although it was more expensive than public transportation, Bella had originally been adamantly opposed to even trying to take a metro bus.

However, out of a desire for Bella to conquer her fears and save money, I took her one Saturday to a public Library and bought us both a bus pass. I then drove home, and we walked to the bus stop closest to our home. Bella and I rode a metro bus together and I showed her how easy it was to get to and from her college.

Bella bravely took the bus home from school just a few nights later; I picked her up in my car at the bus stop after she was dropped off. I could see her walking off the bus in my rearview mirror and she was simply beaming with pride. Bella was proud of herself for standing up to her fear.

Soon after that, I helped Bella apply for a government funded bank card from social services that her intern had told her about which she could use to pay for any extra college expenses (all of her tuition was free), including transportation. That ended my idea of public transportation; the convenient Uber service returned. I really could not blame her for her choice; after all, she was not having to pay for it out of her own money and it was a lot faster than riding a public bus.

Bella did have monthly meetings with her new county social worker. We also heard several times about an Independent Living Program (ILP) coordinator who was supposed to assist Bella in getting her driver's license, a job, etc. However, we never heard from this illusive county ILP coordinator, but our D&M private foster agency's social worker and intern were amazing; they were positive, supportive, consistent, and helped

Bella get her first job in an after-school program for elementary age children. They also encouraged her to start studying for her driver's license test.

Meanwhile, one late afternoon, I opened a letter addressed to Dave and me from our FFA. It was a copy of Bella's annual report, written for a judge by the county social worker she had originally been assigned to under the SILP program; this was the same man who did not think being in our foster home could benefit Bella in any way. The letter was addressed to me, so I opened and read it. I was told the next day on the phone that the FFA had made a mistake sending it to me but had not realized it at the time. They were informed by the county worker that since Bella was 19 years old, as an adult her communications were confidential.

Well, it was too late; I had already read Bella's report and I was not happy about it either. The county social worker described in great detail all of the many things he claimed he had accomplished for Bella, such as getting her California I.D. Card, signing her up for college classes, and buying her a laptop computer (all the things Dave and I had actually done with Bella). I certainly did not need public recognition, but the social worker was flagrantly lying. I called and told Bella's current CSW about the discrepancies, but she was obviously not interested in talking about it and so I let it go.

Bella appeared very happy and had greatly advanced in just a few months, so I suggested to her and her social workers that she might be ready for independent living soon. Although Dave and I were not in a hurry for Bella to leave, I had learned that if foster youths were not accepted into a low rent transitional housing program by the time they were 21 years old, then it was almost impossible to find openings due to the tremendous shortages. Bella was getting close to her 20th birthday and I wanted to help make sure she had a plan set in place to ensure a smooth path for her in the next few years. Her CSW said she would start looking for an opening.

I thought most things were positively progressing with Bella. Little did I know, however, that she had been harboring secrets from us for several months. Our other foster youth, Delores, who had joined us two months after Bella, was pressuring her to keep these secrets for her.

Nineteen-year-old Delores moved into our home after my husband and I were told by her county social worker that Delores had been kicked out of her last foster family's home and had been sleeping in her car. We were also told that the teen's primary needs were a safe bed to sleep in and dental work; poor dental hygiene had been a common denominator with all of our foster kids. Delores was the antithesis of Bella in temperament: talkative, driven, and bold. Her CSW had been working with Delores for 2-½ years and the feisty, pretty Latina already had a job as well as many friends who kept her busy. She even enjoyed cooking for herself, but only ate with us twice in the time she lived with us.

Delores was so busy, in fact, we hardly ever saw her. At the end of the first week having her in our home, I told her county worker and FFA worker that Delores seemed to belong in an independent living program. There were not only very few reasons Delores showed that she needed or wanted to be part of our foster family, but she was also not following our explicit rules.

Delores' FFA and CSW had both told us that since our foster youths were adults, they could basically come and go as they pleased, but that we could establish our basic house rules. Dave and I often felt perplexed over the expectation that we keep these two foster young adults safe in our home, but how they could really do whatever they wanted (thereby making it nearly impossible for us to actually ensure their safety).

Our house rules were the following:

1. Tell us where you are at night and the approximate time that you plan to come home, so we know you are safe.
2. Keep your room and bathroom clean; do your own laundry.
3. Communicate openly and show respect to all family members.
4. Do not smoke or use any alcohol or drugs in our home or yard.
5. You can invite friends over only when either Dave and I are home, and they cannot spend the night.

The social workers approved our house rules and both girls agreed to our terms, but Bella ended up being the only one who followed them. We literally saw Delores a meager 10 minutes out of every week; she would show-up in the middle of the night while Dave and I were sleeping and never communicate anything about her schedule with us. Her side of the bedroom was a heaping mess of clothes, shoes, and makeup; I felt sorry for her tidy roommate, Bella. Furthermore, my super strength nose smelled pungent pot and nicotine several times after Delores moved in, so I reminded her again of our rules and asked her to wash all of her clothes. I also told Delores' new FFA social worker who confronted the young lady on several occasions and even arranged a meeting with all of us; her county worker joined us by telephone. Delores vowed to do better in communicating with us and following our rules.

I did successfully get Delores to numerous needed dental appointments and a long overdue physical. We were told by her CSW that the previous foster parents had not attempted to follow through on any of these requests. Once again, I could not fathom why Dave and I seemed to be required to complete tasks as foster parents that others seemed to get away with ignoring. However, at Delores' physical exam, she refused to take a drug screening test; when I informed the CSW and FFA workers, I was told that since she was an adult and we could not mandate that she take one. I reminded them and Delores that if Dave or I found out that she was taking any illegal substances at our home, that she would have to go. Delores promised that she was not.

Delores could be very sweet. Although I did not think she belonged in a foster family home, she was very likeable. Moreover, she did make a few attempts to inform me of her late arrivals, but her misbehavior continued and even worsened.

One day, Delores decided to quit her job. She talked a blue streak about finding another one, but for two months Dave and I saw no solid evidence that she was doing anything other than being gone at all odd hours of the day and night with her new boyfriend. Delores had been attending a community college before coming to us but had failed her classes; she talked about all of the ideas she had on how she was going to re-enroll and careers she might pursue. However, again, we did not witness any follow through.

I brought up our concerns to Delores' FFA social worker several times and was nicely told that they were supporting the teen while she was working on getting things together. Right before the Covid-19 virus closures, Delores did finally get another job, but I was told by her social worker that she only showed up one day out of the entire week.

Bella and Delores appeared to get along well, despite their differences. However, I had no idea of the manipulation and intimidation Delores was placing on Bella, nor how badly she had been flagrantly abusing our hospitality. It was all made clear to me on Wednesday, March 11, 2020, just two days before California State shut down most public establishments due to the Covid-19 virus epidemic. I was on a field trip with some other staff members and our school's 11th grade students at Home Boy Industries, an extraordinary gang intervention and job training program in Downtown Los Angeles.

I had just opened a bakery fresh turkey and cheese sandwich when the cell phone buzzed in my pocket. I looked at the phone number and realized it was the girls' FFA social worker, so I thought I better answer it. I excused myself and walked outside. The social worker said she was on speaker phone with her supervisor and the intern; the intern said she had just been meeting with our foster daughter, Bella, and that she had told her something that I needed to hear right away. Bella had told her that she had been covering for Delores, but just couldn't do it anymore. She felt badly about keeping secrets from Dave and I, and uncomfortable with Delores' actions. The intern went on to inform me that Bella said that Delores had been vaping, smoking marijuana, and doing harder drugs inside their bedroom in our home; she had also been inviting friends in to do drugs when Dave and I were at work, and had her boyfriend sleepover at least once.

My immediate response was to tell them that Delores would have to be out of our home that evening, because I no longer felt safe having her there. My second response was to feel profoundly hurt. Although I was not very shocked that Delores had lied to us, I still felt like she had abused our love and trust. You would think I would have known better by then with all of the challenged teens I had taught and the experiences Dave and I had with our own adopted son, but I had assumed the best with Delores. I told the social workers that if Delores did not show up that evening at our home to pack her things, Dave and I would do so for her and put everything outside behind our gate.

We hung up and I called my husband to let him know about the situation. We both agreed that he would leave his Track team practice early in the hands of another coach, and head home. He would be able to get there faster than I would, since I was still in Downtown L.A.

After work, Dave went to Walmart and bought huge plastic storage boxes with wheels to assist Delores in packing her things. She had a lot and nothing to put it in. We had always thought it was ridiculous that none of our foster children owned suitcases; they would pitifully pack everything in big, black, plastic trash bags.

After I was finally able to get home that afternoon, Dave and I heard from the FFA social worker several times; she said she had not heard back from Delores yet. So, we started packing up her piles of possessions ourselves. The FFA worker said she would be over later after work to record all of Delores' things, so that the youth could not later claim that we had kept anything from her; that took about 3 long hours. Additionally, the FFA social worker had been unsuccessful in reaching the CSW although she had left multiple voice mail messages.

Finally, at about 9 p.m., when Dave and I were returning from walking our dogs, Delores showed up with her boyfriend to transport her things. She walked past me and said, "I hope you have a wonderful life." There was no apology, not that I expected one. I wondered if her new boyfriend's family was aware that he was dating a young woman with an addiction problem.

I replied to Delores, "Thanks, you too," then walked with Dave and our dogs into our home. It really was not an appropriate time for me to have a conversation with her; I was not ready. Our tired, sweet FFA social worker was still there recording Delores' items too, in the dark, with a flashlight and chair we had provided her.

Fortunately, for Delores, the D&M workers were able to move her temporarily into their own emergency housing until her county worker could find an opening in... wait for it...an independent living program (ILP). The CSW was finally being forced to find an all elusive housing opening for Delores; she had no choice now.

We also had a closure meeting at the FFA a few days after Delores left our home. The teen chose not to come. Our D&M social worker, the intern, an FFA supervisor, and Dave and I chatted for about 15 minutes while we waited for the county worker to arrive. The FFA workers displayed sympathy regarding our feelings of betrayal and safety concerns.

Conversely, the CSW, after she finally arrived at the meeting, showed absolutely no remorse or concern for Dave or I at all. I found myself getting angrier as the CSW painted Delores as the victim in our situation; she said how unjust this was for Delores, since she was now homeless again. I was thinking that there was zero chance that the CSW was unaware of Delores' substance abuse, if she had been on her caseload for over two years; I also started wondering if Delores' last foster parents had really kicked Delores out for the very same reasons we had, not because they were "mean" and "unfair", as they had been described to us.

The true facts were that Delores was not homeless, Dave and I were actually the ones who had been treated unjustly, and now the CSW was going to have to work harder to finally find an

ILP opening for Delores, something I had been suggesting since the first day I had met the youth. I asked how the CSW thought it was fair or safe for not just us, our dogs, and our house, but for sweet, shy Bella, to have Delores behaving that way in our home. Was anyone concerned about the further trauma Bella had endured? Dave and I did wish Bella had told us about Delores' nefarious actions much earlier, but we really did not blame her.

I was more hurt than angry with Delores, but did place culpability in the hands of the adult in the situation who should have known and behaved better: her county social worker. I remarked in the meeting that it appeared to me that Delores obviously had some mental health and substance abuse issues and suggested that maybe she should be required to take a drug test as well as be enrolled in a drug treatment program. I was reminded again that Delores was an adult and although therapy had been offered to her recently and she had not taken advantage of it, no one could demand that she do anything. I stopped wasting my breath, but hoped that Delores would not end up as one of the 20,000 plus failed foster youths who end up living homeless on the streets of America as adults after they no longer receive any government subsidies (Fowler et al. 2017).

After a few minutes, Dave and I were politely excused from the exit meeting for Delores and the social workers remained to finish up. We went home to a clean, peaceful, safe, and drug free home once again; that was March 12, 2020, exactly one day before most of our state closed due to the Corona-19 Virus. We thanked God for the fortuitous timing of Delores' departure, at least for us. We had also had a conversation with Bella that night. She apologized for keeping secrets and my husband and I reassured her that we did not blame her. She seemed relieved.

However, I soon started noticing Bella regressing to former unhealthy behaviors she had displayed when she had first joined us; she was once again staying alone in her bedroom all day and eating very little. She would only hangout with me when we went grocery shopping. It was as if the stress Bella had endured with Delores had flipped a switch in her emotional panel and she was going into a withdrawal mode to cope. The social workers continued to reach out to her, and I shared my concerns.

What made matters worse during the virus closure was that the county mandated that all foster children had to stay quarantined, including Bella (although she was an adult). Bella was not allowed to leave our home to see her siblings or friends and by that time, her school and job had already been closed. Understandably, Bella grew increasingly frustrated, so much so that without any discussion with me, Bella called her county worker and told her that she wanted to return to the SILP program so that she could move back into her uncle's home with one of her sisters. I told Bella that I understood her need for freedom and hoped the transition would be good for her. I also told her that I would still be available for support if she wanted it. Bella lived with us one day and then was gone the next.

Honestly, I was not sure that Dave and I would ever hear from or see Bella again. I was so used to countless, permanent goodbyes with our foster children and my foster/probation students, that I expected it to happen again. I was not so worried about Bella; she had come a long way and I knew she was going to be okay. What took me by surprise was how sad I felt. I did not realize how much I had emotionally attached to Bella. Nonetheless, Bella had decided to leave and I did not want to put any pressure on her, so decided to leave any future contact up to her.

About 3 weeks later, I received a short, sweet text message from Bella. It said, "Hi, Julie. I miss you dearly."

After a big smile and a prayer of thanks, I texted back, "Thanks, Bella! That means a lot to me; I was not sure I was going to hear from you again. I miss you too."

Bella was not finished. Next, she texted me, "You are the best human created, ever."

After a shocked pause and another huge smile, I thanked Bella again.

We ended our conversation by making plans for me to pick Bella up and take her out for lunch a few weeks later with masks, in a drive through, and then eating it on a picnic bench at a park nearby. I was relieved that our relationship had not just abruptly ended; the time and effort Dave and I had spent investing in our foster daughter could still continue, on Bella's terms.

About six months later, Bella admitted to me that she was unhappy in her uncle's home; her younger siblings had moved back in and her uncle expected her to take care of them. The two younger children were home all day due to online Distance Learning and Bella wanted to live her own adult life. Dave and I then helped her move into a room for rent in a nice home near us and a two-block walk away from her best friend.

After Bella left our home, Dave and I decided it was an appropriate time for us to take another break from fostering. I had been offered a position as a middle school assistant principal, something I had been seeking for three years; we knew I would be busy. I still loved being a mom, but knew I was entering a different season, at least for the time being. On the other hand, I warned my sweet husband that I was not closing the door permanently to foster care; it might still be a possibility in the future.

Well, just a few months later, I just happened to get "the itch" to investigate school-age children in the Los Angeles County DCFS system who were already looking to be adopted. I stumbled on a privately run program online called, "KIDSAVE", which worked closely with DCFS. I learned that KIDSAVE was unique in that it actually publicly promoted these children and the children themselves chose which adults with whom they wanted to get to know for possible adoption.

Dave and I had another one of my, "I have an idea, Honey", moments; he agreed to sit with me through an hour long Zoom session in which county social workers displayed pictures of seven children and told their stories. They were surprisingly open about the children's pasts and any medical, intellectual, emotional, or behavioral concerns. After about 30 minutes of taking notes and grabbing more than one tissue, Jackson appeared on the screen. He was a handsome, Black, 11-year old boy who loved school and just wanted to be adopted by a Christian couple; I looked at Dave and said, "I don't need to hear anything more; that's him".

We completed a questionnaire that evening remarking that we wanted to get to know Jackson better. However, we only received silence for two weeks. I finally emailed our contact person at KIDSAVE and asked what was happening in the process. She said she would get back to me.

Another two weeks passed and I had started moving on emotionally, yet, we suddenly received a phone call from KIDSAVE asking Dave and I were still interested in adopting Jackson. I replied, "Yes", but wondered what had been taking place in the previous month. I learned that Jackson had been meeting with another possible placement family, but had decided that they were not a good match for him in terms of a permanent adoption. Now, out of the 80 people who had attended the KIDSAVE event the night that we had heard about Jackson, he had decided he wanted to meet us. Thus began another fostering to adopt adventure.

PART FOUR

Is the Journey Worth It?

Is the Journey Worth It?

Is making a commitment to being a foster or adoptive parent worth it? It depends. Like most things, the answer to that question really depends on the perspective chosen.

These helpless, marginalized children would resolutely say that loving, quality foster care is worth it. Take a minute to imagine the fear, anxiety and anger at being a four, seven, or sixteen-year-old and having a social worker with a police escort suddenly show up to forcibly remove him from the only family he has ever known. Even worse, maybe this is the fifth time he has been removed.

Or, imagine being a teen girl who ran away from her abusive parents and now finds herself homeless, living on the streets, or moving from one friend's couch to another. How much stress is she under? When was the last time she even got a good night's sleep? What kind of fragile self-esteem is she carrying around every day when she tries really hard to hide her homelessness at school among her peers?

Furthermore, how would it feel to be a youth who is the first person in his family to graduate from high school, but now that he has reached age 18, he is forced to leave his group home? He does not have one single adult in the "outs" who gives a damn about what he does next. He wonders what good there is in having dreams if there is no one with whom to share them.

Conversely, how would it feel to be a foster or probation youth who has a social worker fortunate enough to find a caring foster parent and a safe, clean home with a bath and plenty of food for everyone? What if, instead of alcohol induced swearing and yelling, people talk in calm voices and sometimes even laugh in that new home? What if she can finally close her eyes and go to sleep, like, totally sleep, without one eye open, no longer having to be afraid of the monster entering her bedroom in the dark shadows of the night? What if she can almost feel like her new parents like her and might even enjoy having her around? What if, instead of a feeling of complete abandonment, she starts to get an inkling of what it means to have a "support system"?

Although I deeply wish my husband and I could have permanently adopted our foster babies from a decade ago, I do not regret a single moment of the loving care we provided them during perhaps the most crucial time in their lives. There is an abundance of scientific research which supports the idea that the first three years of a child's life are the most important in terms of his/her cognitive, emotional, and social development (Ages and Stages 2019). In fact, the Rauch Foundation (a family foundation based in Long Island, New York, which invests in early intervention in children to promote their success), has determined that, "...85 percent of a person's brain is developed by the time they are five years old" (Why The 2020). Coincidentally, the highest rate for child abuse is also for those under one year old (Child Abuse 2019). Infants all over this country desperately need a safe foster home, even if only temporarily.

Our country desperately needs modern day heroes: caring, selfless adults of all different ages, genders, personalities, ethnicities, and backgrounds, who are willing to parent or mentor traumatized children from foster care and juvenile probation from ages birth to 18, or even up to 21 in some states. Yes, it is a risky step, but does not everything worthwhile in life involve taking risks? The profound difference that can be made in the lives of at-risk children, be it in seemingly insignificant or life-changing acts, might not only bring healing, but also create a new, healthy pattern of lifestyle choices for future generations.

However, in terms of fostering and adopting, what do the foster parents get out of it, besides the knowledge that they have made an immeasurable difference? It is certainly not any noticeable monetary gain. At $1,000/month per child, up to age 18, for foster parents or adoptive parents in L.A. County, they will be lucky if this stipend just covers the child's expenses. This is especially true if they take in infants or older teenagers (AAP 2020), who have greater daily living expenses.

Yes, foster care can be viewed as a practical business relationship in which the parents are meeting a need for which social services compensates them. I am not so naive to think that every foster parent has a bleeding heart like mine. Yet, I know for sure that the foster or adopted child will easily be able to determine a parent's motivations; they are just smart like that. They had to be remarkably savvy to survive previous years of manipulation, abuse, and rejection by adults who said they loved them. So, I beg adults who enter foster care to do so with a primary goal of being to provide ongoing unconditional love, safety, visits with their biological families, healthcare, educational support, physical activity, attention, discipline, nutritious meals, baked cookies, playtime, finger painting, birthday parties, museum visits, dance or music lessons, swim lessons, hugs, laughter, toys, puppies, new clothes, social outlets, and all of the other ingredients to a happy childhood. In other words, to treat a foster or adopted child as one of the family, not as a guest. Foster children will notice the difference from the moment they walk through the front doorway.

Furthermore, foster, probation, or adoptive youths might just give their caregivers unconditional love in return. Regardless of what the children give or do not give back, foster parents' perspectives on life will definitely be changed forever. It might even impact others around them. I end the story of my journey thus far with reflections of those who have travelled closest with me on this journey, my husband and our two adult children.

Dave, My Husband

Hundreds of thousands of kids are in the child welfare system. I see them in my classroom and sometimes meet them as adults who came through the system in their childhoods years earlier. Our journey as foster parents has taught me to never assume others had the loving upbringing I had. For many, "home" is not a good place or a positive memory. For instance, relationships I might take for granted, like grandparents, are a cherished and rare commodity for many foster children.

Additionally, the L.A. County child welfare system never seems to improve, but the private foster family agencies (FFAs), try to bring a caring and common-sense approach to the process. When it comes to the system, birth parents may not be a healthy plan for the child's future and the system cannot seem to let this idea go. Damaged parents don't always recover, and the kids need to be the priority. Every child needs a family and "family" may have nothing to do with birth parents. Your family is who loves and raises you, who attends your games and events, and who is there when things go wrong.

I also discovered through fostering how critical attachment is in the first years of life, even if that attachment is provided by nurturing foster parents who will not see the child grow up in the long run. Except for our adopted son, Jacob, what we did in raising other people's children meant we would not get to see them grow up or share in their years ahead. This was and still is hard for me. I sometimes think of all our little ones; I pray for them and I wonder where they are, what they look like now. I hope they are healthy and safe. I hope that I had an impact on them and made their lives better.

I will never forget watching Baby Anna cry out and grow panicked when she met her forever, adoptive family. She needed to hear my voice and be held by me to calm down. Anna had attached to us and she knew us well, even in the four short months we cared for her. Letting go of these precious little ones was painful; seeing some of them go back to their previous environments was wrenching.

Most people have no clue how the system really works. Many just seem glad someone else is offering to be a foster parent. Likewise, these same people are awfully nosy when they see foster families and want to ask intrusive personal questions.

Lastly, I have learned that adoption is an amazing process. The child becomes a full member of his/her family. The newly created birth certificate is a tangible indicator of a fresh start for the child's life. The judge in an adoption ceremony even emphasizes that future financial equity is expected to be a part of the child's inclusion into the family.

Jacob, Our Adopted Son

I can remember how I felt when new foster children joined our family well. I was the one you guys adopted, but I had *a lot of confusion. It was as if I thought this next child was going to take my place, but after a while I became okay with it. I mean, you guys were/are my parents and I never had someone to call mine, so when someone else came along I felt threatened. I never said anything, but yeah, it made me feel that way.*

Alisa, Julie, Jacob, & Dave McKissick

As I got older, I realized you guys were just trying to help someone like me and I became simi-okay with it. I was selfish about my family; I did not have one before, so I was extra defensive. Although, I was also always excited for someone new to come into the house.

I would tell foster parents to not expect their children to get along right away with the new foster children. Kids take it as competition, unless there is a lot of reassurance; you guys were always good at reassuring me that you loved me and wanted to help someone in a situation like I'd been in. That is what kinda changed my view on it, but I came from a foster family (before you), who'd always bring new kids in and it was always a negative thing. I'd be pushed to the side, kinda, especially with younger babies; they didn't care about me once they came.

I felt like it was going to happen the same way at your house. but you'd remind me that I was your child and you guys loved me as one. I wasn't just another good deed. Like, you actually showed me love and affection. as if I was your own. So, after a while, I was okay with having other kids in our home. But, it got kinda crazy, after Miguel (referring to our five year old foster son), and I was really over it. I couldn't take it.

I wish I'd been older then, so that I could have taken everything in a little more and realized how we could have helped Miguel. He could have been a good kid. To be honest, I feel like I didn't help as far as trying to be an older brother to Miguel. I just never saw it like that at the time, which is sad; I was still worried about me because that's all I grew up worrying about".

I'm also lucky Alisa accepted me; the older brother and sister at my last foster home would ignore me and treat me as if I was temporary. Alisa is amazing".

Alisa, Our Daughter

I think the main way that being a foster sister impacted me was that it broadened my perspective. It helped me see how different people grow up in very different circumstances and environments, and how those can affect their opportunities in life. Fostering made me appreciate everything that I had, including seemingly simple things, like my safety, because our foster kids did not have it. Conversely, it made me angry that there was such a discrepancy and made me want to change the lives of other kids in some way.

At first, I told my mom I wanted to be a judge, so that I

could make sure foster kids didn't have to go back to horrific family situations. But, my passion for social justice and kids later materialized into teaching in South Los Angeles. Becoming a teacher in a poverty-stricken neighborhood is probably not something I ever would have thought of doing if it hadn't been for the tiny lives I helped care for.

In broadening my perspective, I think foster care also helped me relate to people better. I was very introverted as a child but caring for babies and kids from a young age forced me into a leadership role of sorts. It helped me mature and show patience to others. Growing up with my brother particularly taught me the importance of patience. Most people could say the same when it comes to siblings, but to learn to not only tolerate Jacob, but also accept and love him was a process.

Alisa with Grandma & Grandpa Reed

It was a beneficial process and if it were not for experiences like these, I don't know if I would have been shaped into a more patient and understanding adult. Understanding people's backgrounds and personal histories helps us better understand the people themselves and the choices they make. Fostering helped me see people in a different way, not just as a product of the choices they make. It opened my eyes to the inequity that exists in our nation, in our state, and even within a single city or town.

Special Appreciation

Thank you, Dad and Mom Reed, for taking a chance on me and starting this journey. Dave, my dependable husband, thank you for being my amazing traveling partner. Thank you, Alisa, our sweet daughter, for sharing our attention, your bedroom, your heart, and even your inheritance with numerous little ones along the way. Thank you to our other family members and friends who provided sustenance for our journey and contributed to the writing of this book. My great appreciation goes out to those extraordinary educators, social workers, probation officers, and counselors standing on the frontlines across America who provide safety for abused, neglected, and profoundly troubled children on their journeys with integrity. I also extend my profound thanks and kinship to other foster parents. Most of all, I thank God, my Father in heaven, who did not count my humble beginnings against me, but instead called me to be a Mama Bear to America's most marginalized children.

Resources

"About Us." *WestEd: Improving Learning, Healthy Development, and Equity in Schools and Communities*, WestEd.org, 26 May 2020, www.wested.org/about-us/.

"Adoptions Assistance Program (AAP)." *California Department of Social Services (CDSS)*, 2020, www.cdss.ca.gov/adoptions-assistance.

"Ages and Stages of Development." *Ages and Stages of Development – Child Development (CA Dept of Education)*, California Department of Education, 24 June 2019, www.cde.ca.gov/sp/cd/re/caqdevelopment.asp.

Agrawal, Nina. "Youth Housing Program Shut Down Amid Probes." *Los Angeles Times*, 16 Dec. 2019.

Ahlin, Eileen M. "Ending Sexual Assault in Youth Detention Centers." *The Conversation*, 4 July 2019, theconversation.com/ending-sexual-assault-in-youth-detention-centers-92336.

Alvarez, Frank. "Giving Gangs L.I.P.: Dealing with Gangs as a Foster Parent." *Embrella Blog*, 27 Apr. 2016, foster-adoptive-kinship-family-services-nj.org/fosterparents-and-gangs/.

Americashealthrankings.org. United Health Foundation, 2020.

American Adoptions, Inc. "'What Does Adoption Mean to a Child?'." *American Adoptions - Being Adopted - A Look at the Happiness of Children Growing Up Adopted*, American Adoptions, 2020.

Anders, Sean, director. *Instant Family*. Paramount Pictures,
        2018. "Assembly Bill No. 216." *Bill Text - AB-216 High School
        Graduation Requirements: Pupils in Foster Care.*, California
        Legislature, 23 Sept. 2013.

Babbel, Susanne. "The Foster Care System and Its Victims:
        Part 2." *Psychology Today*, Sussex Publishers, 3 Jan. 2012.

Bianco, Margery Williams, and Florence Graham. *The
        Velveteen Rabbit, or, How Toys Become Real*. Grosset & Dunlap,
        Pub., 1996.

Boyle, Father Gregory. "Thought for the Day: Hope Never
        Gets Old." *YouTube,* uploaded by Homeboy Industries, 27, April
        2020, https://www.youtube.com/watch?v=7ZgavyQ-jjc&t=3s.

California Department of Social Services (CDSS). PDF, "All
        County Letter No. 16-79". CDSS, 22 Sept., 2016.

California Department of Social Services (CDSS). PDF, "All
        County Letter No. 17-122". CDSS, 9 Jan. 2018.

California Department of Social Services (CDSS). PDF,
        "Resource Family Home Health and Safety Assessment Checklist".
        CDSS, 19 July, 2020.

California Department of Social Services (CDSS). PDF,
        "Short Term Residential Therapeutic Program Interim Licensing
        Standards, Chapter 7.5, Version 3". CDSS, 11 Jan. 2019.

California Foster Youth Education Task Force (CFYETF).
        PDF, "California Foster Youth Education Law Facts Sheets". CFYETF,
        7th Edition, June, 2019.

"California Hopes to Place More Probation Youth in Foster
        Homes Like This." *The Chronicle of Social Change*, 22 Feb. 2018.

"California Law-Welfare and Institutions Code: Chapter1,
        Foster Care Placement-California Law 16000-16014." *California
        Legislature Information*, California Legislature, 1 Jan. 2020.

"Camp Erwin Owen." *Camp Erwin Owen*, Kern County
Probation, 2013.

Cdnadmin. "To What Degree Do the Criminal Justice and
Child Welfare Populations in California Overlap?" *Children's Data
Network*, CDN, 6 June 2017.

"CDSS Programs: Reasonable and Prudent Parent
Standard." *California Department of Social Services*, 2020.

Center for Public Policy Studies (CPPS). PDF, "California
Human Trafficking Fact Sheet". CPPS. Feb. 2013.

Cherry, Kendra, LCSW. "Permissive Parenting
Characteristics and Effects." Very well Mind, 15 Aug. 2019.

"Child Abuse Statistics." *American Society for the Positive
Care of Children*, SPCC, 18
Dec. 2019, americanspcc.org/child-abuse-statistics/.

"Child Poverty." *NCCP*, Bank Street Graduate School of Education, 2019.

Child Trends. PDF, "California: Adoption from Foster Care".

"Children in Foster Care by Age Group: KIDS COUNT Data
Center." *KIDS COUNTData Center: A Project of the Annie E. Casey
Foundation*, Annie E. Casey Foundation, Mar. 2020.

Children's Bureau. PDF, "Foster Care Statistics 2017". Childwelfare.gov, 2017.

Children's Bureau-Child Welfare. PDF, "Parental Substance
Abuse and the Child Welfare System". childwelfare.gov, Oct, 2014.

Children's Law Center of California (CLCCAL). PDF, "Know Before
You Go: Supervised Independent Living Placement
(SILP)". CLCCAL, 2013.

"Chola." *Urban Dictionary*, 16 Apr. 2007,
www.urbandictionary.com/define.php?term=chola.

Cinahl Information Systems. PDF, "Children with Developmental
    Disabilities: Issues in Foster Care and Adoption in the
    United States". 15 July 2016.

Commercially Sexually Exploited Children (CSEC). PDF, "CSEC
    Leadership Team Quarterly Report". L.A.County.gov, 2018.

County of Los Angeles. PDF, "County of Los Angeles Department
    of Children and Family Services and Probation
    Department Short-term Residential Therapeutic
    Programs Foster Care Placement Services Contract". 02 Jan. 2018.

Coyle, Sue. "Children with Intellectual Disabilities in Foster Care." *Social Work
    Today*, Nov. 2014, p. 22.

Curtis, J. L., & Cornell, L. (1998). *Tell Me Again About the Night I
    Was Born*. New York, NY: HarperCollins.

D'Agostino, John Osborn. "About EdSource." *EdSource.org*,
    EdSource, 24 Sept. 2019, edsource.org/about-edsource.

Daniels, Jeff. "California Plan Aims to Slash State's Child Poverty
    Rate in Half by 2039." *CNBS.com*, 11 Apr. 2019.

Danielson, Caroline, and Helen Lee. PDF, "Foster Care in
    California: Achievements and Challenges". Public Policy
    Institute of California, 2010.

Day, Brian. "Pomona Police Rescue 3rd Teenage Human
    Trafficking Victim in 2 Weeks." *KTLA*, KTLA, 1 Sept. 2019.

De Victoria, S. L., Ph.D. (2018, July 08). Emotional Trauma in the
    Womb. Retrieved June 18, 2020.

"Drug Rehab Success Rates and Statistics." *American Addiction
    Centers*, 19 May 2020, americanaddictioncenters.org/rehab-
    guide/success-rates-and-statistics.

Education Outcomes for Kids in Foster Care. Leg.state.nv, 2018.

"11 Facts About Child Abuse." *DoSomething.org*, 2015.

"Facts about Down Syndrome." *Centers for Disease Control and Prevention*, Centers for Disease Control and Prevention, 5 Dec. 2019.

"Facts & Stats." *Alliance for Children's Rights*, 15 May 2019, kids alliance.org/facts-stats/.

"Facts on Foster Care in America." *ABC News*, ABC News Network, 12 Sept. 2006, abcnews.go.com/Primetime/FosterCare/story?id=2017 991&page=1.

Farmer, Liz. "Fighting Sex Trafficking Is Harder Than It Seems." *Governing*, Jan. 2017.

Feizi, Awat et al. "Parenting stress among mothers of children with different physical, mental, and psychological problems." *Journal of research in medical sciences: the official journal of Isfahan University of Medical Sciences* vol. 19,2 (2014):145-52.

Fitton, Victoria A. PDF, "Childhood Attachment Disorder/Disruption: A Symptom Checklist". Michigan State University, 18 May, 2020.

"Foster Care Bill of Rights." *Foster Care Bill of Rights*, National Conference of State Legislatures, 29 Oct. 2019.

"Foster Care Facts." *Children's Law Center of California*, 2014.

"Foster Youth Education Rights." *Foster Youth Education Rights –Foster Youth Services (CA Dept of Education)*, California Department of Education, 3 Dec. 2019.

Foster Youth Help, DSS.CA.GOV. PDF, "The Foster Youth Bill of Rights", 1 Jan 2020.

"Foster Youth in California Schools." *Foster Youth in California Schools - Student Group Information (CA Dept of Education)*, California Department of Education, 20 Apr. 2020.

"14 Days Notice of Placement Change & Grievance Review Hearing - Advokids: A Legal Resource for California Foster Children and Their Advocates." *Advokids*, Advokids.org, 17 Apr. 2020,

Fowler, Patrick J et al. "Homelessness and Aging Out of Foster Care: A National Comparison of Child Welfare-Involved Adolescents." *Children and youth services review* vol. 77 (2017): 27-33. doi:10.1016/j.childyouth.2017.03.017

Getz, Lindsey. "A Closer Look at Family First — The Pros and Cons of Recent Foster Care Legislation." *Social Work Today*, Great Valley Publishing Company, 2020.

Given Place Media (GPM). "Juvenile Halls and Camps-Los Angeles County Probation Department." *Los Angeles Almanac,* 2020, p. 1.

Given Place Media (GPM). "Poverty and Lower Living Income Level Guidelines." *Los Angeles Almanac*, 2020, p. 1.

Grim, Ryan, and Aida Chavez. "Children Are Dying at Alarming Rates in Foster Care, and Nobody Is Bothering to Investigate." *The Intercept*, The Intercept, 18 Oct. 2017, theintercept.com /2017/10/18/foster-care-children-deaths-mentor-network/. "Housing." *Housing | Eastern Los Angeles Regional Center*, ELARC, 2020.

Hammond, Zaretta. *Culturally Responsive Teaching and the Brain: Promoting Authentic Engagement and Rigor among Culturally and Linguistically Diverse Students*. Corwin, a SAGE Company, 2015.

Howell, James. National Criminal Justice, Office of Juvenile Justice Delinquency and Prevention. PDF, "Gang Prevention: An Overview of Research and Programs". NCJ, Dec 2010.

"Human Trafficking." *COUNTY OF LOS ANGELES*, 17 Jan.
2020,lacounty.gov/human-trafficking/.

Lannelli, Vincent. "How Common Is Child Abuse?" *Verywell Mind*,
Verywell Mind, 4 Feb. 2020.

"Increased Risk Groups." *Youth.gov*, 14 June 2020,
youth.gov/youth-topics/youth-suicide- prevention/increased-risk-
groups.

"IFoster." *IFoster*, 2020.

Instant Family. Directed by Sean Anders and Mark Wahlberg,
starring Mark Wahlberg, Paramount Pictures, 16 Nov 2018.

Jacques, Jaime. "States with the Most Children in Foster Care."
Thestacker.com, Stacker, 13 Nov. 2018,
thestacker.com/stories/2034/states-most-children-foster-care.

Johnson, Lacey. "As More Schools Aid Foster Students, Data on
Results Needed, Researchers Say." *Youth Today*, 30 May 2019,
youthtoday.org/2019/03/as-more-colleges-states-aid-youth-in-
foster-care-data-on results-is-needed-researchers-say/.

"Juvenile Delinquency." *Juvenile Delinquency –
juvenile_famlaw_selfhelp*, Judicial Council of California, 2020.

"Juvenile Felony Arrest Rate." *Kidsdata.org*, Lucile Packard
Foundation for Children's Health , May 2019,

Kelly, John, et al. "Fewer Foster Youth, More Foster Homes:
Findings from the 2019 Who Cares Project." *The Chronicle of Social
Change*, 24 Oct. 2019, chronicleofsocialchange.org/featured/less-
foster-youth-more-foster-homes-findins-from-the-2019-who-cares-
project/38197.

King, Martin Luther. "Where Do We Go From Here?"
Plough.com, Plough Publishing House, 15 Jan. 2017.

Lahey, Jessica. "Every Time Foster Kids Move, They Lose Months
of Academic Progress." *The Atlantic*, Atlantic Media
Company, 28 Feb. 2014.

Lawson, Jennifer, et al. "Favoring Reunification for Children in
Foster Care Is a Legal Mandate, Not Bias Against Foster Parents."
The Chronicle of Social Change, The Chronicle of Social Change,
16 May 2017, chronicleofsocialchange.org/opinion/favoring-
reunification-for-children-in-foster care-is-a-legal-mandate-not-bias-
against-foster-parents/26833.

Lipari, Rachel, and Struther L. Van Horn. "Children Living with
Parents Who Have a Substance Use Disorder." *Children Living with
Parents Who Have a Substance Use Disorder*, Substance Abuse and
Mental Health Services Administration (SAMHSA), 24 Aug. 2017.

Los Angeles County Department of Children and Family Services,
DCFS, 2019, dcfs.lacounty.gov/youth/know-your-rights/.

Los Angeles Unified School District. PDF, "Overview of Foster
Care Legislation". 8 August, 2014.

Loxton, Michelle. "Foster Care System Struggles To Implement
New Law." *Kazu.org*, California State University, Monterey Bay, 6
June 2019.

Macías, Jorge. "School Meals: a Reflection of Growing Poverty in
Los Angeles." *CalMatters*, 8 Oct. 2019,
calmatters.org/california-divide/2019/10/school-meals-a-reflection-
of-growing-poverty-in-la/.

Mandell, David. "Why Too Many Children with Autism End up in
Foster Care." *Spectrum*, Simmons Foundation, 9 Jan. 2018.

Mbenque, Nina Williams. PDF, "Social and Emotional Well-being
of Children in Foster Care". 2012.

McCarty, Alyn T. "Child Poverty in the United States: A Tale of
Devastation and the Promise of Hope." *Sociology Compass*, vol. 10,
no. 7, 4   July 2016, pp. 623–639. *National Center for
Biotechnology Information*, doi:10.1111/soc4.12386.

Miller, Caroline. "Mental Health Disorders and Teen Substance
Use." *Child Mind Institute*, 28 Jan. 2020,
childmind.org/article/mental-health-disorders-and-
substance-use/.

Montero, Alexander. "Quick Guide: Students in Foster Care."
EdSource, EdSource, 29 Apr. 2020.

Moore, Catherine. "Shame and the Adopted Child." *Adoptive
Families Association of BC*, Adoptive Families
Association BC, 5 Oct. 2017.

National Council on Crime and Delinquency. PDF, "A Profile of
Youth in the Los Angeles County Delinquency Prevention Pilot".
NCCD, December 2015.

Nelson-Butler, Cheryl, The Racial Roots of Human Trafficking
(2015). UCLA Law Review, Vol. 62, No. 1464, 2015; SMU Dedman
School of Law Legal Studies Research Paper No. 179.

New International Version (NIV) Study Bible. Zondervan, 1985.

Newell, Michelle, and Leap, Jorja. *Reforming the Nation's
Largest Juvenile Justice System*. Children's Defense Fund, 2013,
pp. 1–18.

Nfyiadmin. "51 Useful Aging Out of Foster Care Statistics: Social
Race Media." *National Foster Youth Institute*, 26 May 2017.

North American Council on Adoptable Children (NACAC). PDF,
"New Jersey Adoption Facts". Fall 2014.

Office of Juvenile Justice and Delinquency Prevention (OJJDP).
PDF, "Intersection Between Mental Health and the Juvenile Justice
System". July 2017.

"Open' or 'Closed' Adoption?" *FamilyEducation*, 25 July 2006.

"Our Youth in Need." *Create Now*, 2020.

Palta, R. (2013, August 20). Foster bed shortage straining LA's
        child welfare system. KPCC. Retrieved June 27, 2020.

"Parentherald.com." *Parentherald.com*, Parent Herald, 28 Feb.
        2020.

Park, Madison. "Adopted Children at Greater Risk for Mental
        Health Disorders." *CNN*, Cable News Network, 14 Apr. 2010.

Platt, M. (2020, April 01). California State Adoption Assistance
        Program. Retrieved June 27, 2020.

"POLICY." *0900-511.10, Rates for Placement and Related
        Services*, L.A. County DCFS, 1 July 2019,
        m.policy.dcfs.lacounty.gov/Src/Content/AFDC_FC_GRI_
        FC_Rates.htm.

Rector, Kevin. "Reports of Online Child Sex Abuse Surge Amid
        Pandemic." *Los Angeles Times*, 22 May 2020, pp. A1–A9.

Riley, N. S. (2019, October 17). Opinion: Why 'Sesame Street' is
        smarter about foster care than your local child welfare agency.
        Los Angeles Times. Retrieved June 26, 2020.

Rubin, D. M., et al. "The Impact of Placement Stability on
        Behavioral Well-Being for Children in Foster Care."
        Pediatrics, vol. 119, no. 2, Jan. 2007, pp. 336–344.,
        doi:10.1542/peds.2006-1995.

Russell, Betsy Z. "Twenty Percent Increase Proposed to Idaho's
        Foster Parent Reimbursements." *The Spokesman-Review - Eye on
        Boise*, 31 Jan. 2017.

Sanzo, Kimberly. "Language Deprivation."
    TherapyTravelers.com, TherapyTravelers, 12 Feb. 2019,
    therapytravelers.com/language-deprivation/.
    "The Adoption Assistance and Child Welfare Act of 1980."
    Child and Family Services Reviews, Child and Family Services
    Reviews, 2017, training.cfsrportal.acf.hhs.gov/section-2-
    understanding-child-welfare-system/2998

Schools, Kern County Superintendent of Blanton Education
    Center: Kern County Superintendent of Schools - Office of Mary C.
    Barlow." *Alternative Education*, Kern County Superintendent of
    Schools, 2020, kern.org/alted/community-schools/blanton-
    education-center/.

Sepulveda, Kristin, and Sarah Catherine Williams. "One in Three
    Children Entered Foster Care in 2017 Because of Parental Drug
    Abuse." *Child Trends*, 29 Apr.2020.

Shevlin, Becky, and Nancy Cohen. *Report on the Status of
    Women in Los Angeles County*. LACCW, 2016, pp. 1–36.

"State-by-State Data." *The Sentencing Project*, 2019.

Stiles, Matt. "Danger and Dysfunction in L.A. County Juvenile
    Halls." *Los Angeles Times*, 19 May 2019.

Sullivan, Regina, and Elizabeth Norton Lasley. "Fear in Love:
    Attachment, Abuse, and the Developing Brain." *Cerebrum : the
    Dana Forum on Brain Science*, The Dana Foundation & National
    Center for Biotechnology Information, 1 Sept. 2010.

Teofilo, Debbie. "Camp Owen, the 'Little City.'" *Kern Valley Sun*,
    6 Feb. 2018.

The Nanny. Seasons 1-6, CBS, Columbia TriStar & Sony Pictures,
    3 Nov. 1993-99.

Tiano, Sara, et al. "Hundreds of Trafficked Girls, Thousands of
        Child Welfare Referrals." *The Chronicle of Social Change*, 17 May
        2020, chronicleofsocialchange.org/csec/los-angeles-csec-report-
        child-welfare/32754.

Tucker, Jill, and Joaquin Palomino. "Juvenile Hall Costs
        Skyrocket." *San Francisco Chronicle*, 26 Apr. 2019.

Vaughn, Michael G, et al. "Substance Use and Abuse among
        Older Youth in Foster Care." *Addictive Behaviors*, U.S. National
        Library of Medicine, 2 Feb. 2009.

Washburn, Maureen. "California's Division of Juvenile Justice
        (DJJ) Reports High Recidivism Despite Surging Costs -Center on
        Juvenile and Criminal Justice." *Center on Juvenile and Criminal
        Justice*, Apr. 2017.

Wasson, Valentina Pavlovna. *Chosen Baby*. Lippincott, 1950.

Waters, Rob. "Despite Education Reforms, Foster Students in
        California Lag Far behind on Multiple Measures ."
        EdSource.org, EdSource, 6 Apr. 2019.

Webb, Kerri. "L.A. Completes Facility Consolidation Plan by
        Closing Nine Juvenile Facilities in Two Years." *County of Los Angeles
        Probation*, 9 Aug. 2019, probation.lacounty.gov/l-a-probation-
        completes-facility-consolidation-plan-by-closing-nine-juvenile-
        facilities-in-two-years/.

Wexler, Richard. "Abuse in Foster Care: Research vs. the Child
        Welfare System's Alternative Facts." *Youth Today*, 24 Feb. 2018,
        youthtoday.org/2017/09/abuse-in-foster-care-research-vs-the-child-
        welfare-systems-alternative- facts/.

"Why The First 5 Years of Child Development Are So Important:
        Children's Bureau." *Child Abuse Prevention, Treatment & Welfare
        Services | Children's Bureau*, Children's Bureau, 8 Jan. 2020.

"Why Young People Join Gangs." *Los Angeles Police Department*, 2020.

Wiltz, Teresa. "This New Federal Law Will Change Foster Care As We Know It." *The Pew Charitable Trusts*, 2 May 2018.

Yerby, Nathan. "Drug Addiction Is Sending More Children to Foster Care." *Addiction Center*, 29 Apr. 2020.

Zivanovic, Crista. "Gang Members on Path of 'Assumed Destiny' — Dying by Age 20." *NWI Times*, 5 Feb. 2014.

Made in the USA
Las Vegas, NV
16 July 2021